EAST IS EAST

GEORGE MIKES

EAST IS EAST

*

NICOLAS BENTLEY
drew the pictures

ANDRE DEUTSCH

FIRST PUBLISHED SEPTEMBER 1958 BY
ANDRE DEUTSCH LIMITED
12–14 CARLISLE STREET SOHO SQUARE
LONDON WI
SECOND IMPRESSION OCTOBER 1958

PRINTED IN GREAT BRITAIN BY
TONBRIDGE PRINTERS LIMITED
TONBRIDGE KENT

CONTENTS

LOVE YOUR CONTINENT, HATE YOUR NEIGHBOUR

JAPAN

FORMOSA

CONTENTS

THE PHILIPPINES

HONG KONG

MALAYA

SIAM

INDIA

CONTENTS

INDIA (*continued*)

TURKEY

'East is East and the West is San Francisco . . .'

O. HENRY

LOVE YOUR CONTINENT, HATE YOUR NEIGHBOUR

NO SUCH PLACE AS ASIA

The most important and for me the most surprising discovery I made on my trip to Asia was that there is no such place. The atlas shows indeed a vast land mass called 'Asia', at which, if you proceed in the right direction, you will certainly arrive. But the word 'Asia' is no more than that – a geographical notion. Asia, it is said, is 'another world': if anything, it is twenty other worlds.

I have a vague suspicion that such phrases as 'Asian spirit', 'Asian man', the 'Asian idea' were invented partly by European leader-writers and partly by Asian nationalists. After all, what has a Khirgiz hunter to do with a Japanese geisha girl? Nothing: which I am sure is the Khirgiz hunter's loss. What connection is there between a tailor in Hong Kong and an oil-prospector in Israel? There is far less brotherly feeling between a Persian goat-herd and a Filipino millionaire than there is between the Filipino millionaire and his counterpart in the City of London.

There is not even an Asian type. Of course, a glance at
some people will enable us to say with a reasonable degree
of certainty that they come from Asia. But we are likely to
confuse Japanese with Chinese, Siamese with Indonesians,
Persians with Arabs or Indians, just as many Chinese fail
to discern any difference between a Swede and a Spaniard.
An Asian does not necessarily resemble a fellow-Asian more
than an Eskimo resembles a Cypriot. There are so many
distinct Asian types that the phrase 'Asian man' is almost
completely devoid of meaning.

'Asian problems' is another popular catch-phrase. But
what are we to regard as the 'Asian problems'? Over-
population? It exists in many other countries outside Asia;
Siam and Malaya, on the other hand, are Asian countries
and they are under-populated. Or is 'newly acquired independence' the problem of Asia? But Japan and Siam have
always been independent; certain Asian countries are
independent in name only; and again the problems of independence – even where they are very real – can vary greatly
from one to another. Asia is not republican, although India
is no longer ruled by a queen; nor is it monarchist, although
the monarchy enjoys as high a standing in Siam and Japan
as in any other country of the world and the newly-
born Malaya, too, has chosen a constitutional form of
kingdom.

People like to talk of an 'Asian consciousness' and a 'sense
of unity' among Asians. This is nonsense. The Asians love
their continent but, on the whole, hate their neighbours,
just as ordinary human beings do all over the world. The
average Filipino still turns green at the very mention of
Japan. China is feared, yet admired, hated and loved by all
her neighbours. If Israel could only be forgotten, not much
love would be lost between Syria and Iraq. Or try to discuss
the problem of Kashmir 'objectively' and 'coolly' with an
Indian and a Pakistani. In theory they love one another

as Asians; in practice they would enjoy few things better than cutting one another's throats in the normal, human way.

★   ★   ★

A famous playwright once said to me: 'One can write a book on a country after three days or after thirty years. Nothing can be done in between.' This, I believe, is basically true and as true, of course, about a continent as it is about a single country. It is my painful duty to admit that this book on Asia belongs very much to the three-day category. If the reader cares to know what I saw and thought, he is cordially invited to accompany me; but if he wants to know what Asia is really like, then . . . well, then he is lost. There is no way of finding out. Because, I repeat, Asia does not exist; it has only been invented. In the following pages you can contemplate the Asia *I* have invented.

ETIQUETTE FOR EUROPEANS

In Asia it is not done to speak of the 'Far East', the 'East', the 'Middle East', etc. This is due partly to common sense and partly to the over-sensitiveness of Asians. The Japanese do not mind it. Indeed, they call their country the Land of the Rising Sun; but the Indians – led by Mr Nehru in this respect, too – do strongly object.

It would be really absurd for a Japanese to think of his home as 'here, in the Far East'. You could almost make a metaphysical problem out of it: how can one be 'here', yet, at the same time 'in the Far East'. What they are far from is of course Europe and it is exactly this Europe-centred way of looking at things that so-called 'orientals' resent. Why should an Indian speak of the Middle East which is West of him? For a Japanese, surely, New York ought to be the Far East, not Tokyo. The traditional phraseology must be just as objectionable to Australians and Americans as Asians. To Australians Japan is not the Far East but the Near North; a Californian has to travel westward to reach the East and why should a man from Oregon call Cairo the Middle East if he calls Kansas City the Middle West? South-East Asia, Western Asia, Eastern Asia, are purely relative notions.

If the logical case is so strong, you may ask, where does the over-sensitiveness of the Asians come in? It comes in when you endeavour to point out to them that, in spite of all this, the meridian does run through Greenwich. It does, indeed – they may reply – but why? Simply because the meridian is a hireling of the Imperialists. It ought to run through New Delhi or, at least, Ghana. It has certainly no business to run through a suburb of London. Maybe they are right, after all: and as soon as Europe has ceased to be the centre of the universe, the Far East will have ceased to be the Far East and the meridian, too, should be handed over either to the United States for safe keeping or to India to show that we do understand the spirit of modern times.

Then again, never call an Asian an 'Asiatic'. I did not quite understand why, so they explained to me that it carries a slightly contemptuous connotation. It never had for me. In fact, I vaguely remembered from my erstwhile classical studies that the Romans used the word 'Asiaticus' as a geographical notion, while the word 'Asianus' – brought into usage at a later period – somewhat disparagingly, referred to the most backward part of their Empire. But this etymological argument is neither here nor there. Give a man the name he wants. In England there are plenty of names like Cholmondeley, pronounced *Chumley*. You do not argue with Mr Cholmondeley over this. Or take my name, Mikes. You do not argue with me that since it is spelt M-I-K-E-S, it must clearly rhyme with 'likes'. As soon as I explain – however diffidently – that I call myself Mee-cash, you shrug your shoulders, think what you like, and call me Mee-cash. (By the way, Asian 'flu meant a great though not total victory in this field. It is true that hardly anyone speaks of 'Asiatic 'flu'; but the Russians – as no bad thing may come, at least in their present mood, from Asia – keep calling it Australian 'flu. I think the Australians ought to retaliate and call it Russiatic 'flu.)

You must never speak of 'white men' either. You call Europeans Europeans. So far so good. In a civilised world people should not be classified by their colour: and to call white men 'Europeans' is very sensible indeed, except for the somewhat surprising consequence that Americans, Australians and New Zealanders thus become Europeans, too. In this connection I made a bold and revolutionary suggestion: what about calling Americans *Americans*? And Australians *Australians*? My suggestion was politely but firmly turned down as extravagant and over-complicated.

COLONIALISM

'Colonialism' is one of the best hated words in Asia. As a result of constant propaganda it has become an almost meaningless term of abuse and in some cases, as ugly a word as 'peace' and 'democracy' when printed in *Pravda*. Of course, it has never been a pretty word and I am not going to try to defend it. But there is much more to it than meets the eye.

Colonialism is, first of all, an insult. That is why it is rejected so emotionally by all Asians. It is not so much the economic aspects of colonialism that cause the real hard feelings; it is the implied slur. It all boils down to this: 'You are not mature and intelligent enough to govern yourself so we shall come along and govern you.' This is indeed insulting. But however insulting, nevertheless, one thing does not follow, namely, that all nations are, in fact, able to govern themselves. This is just one more example of the regrettable untidiness of things. The reverse of wrong is not always right; the reverse of a lie is not always the truth.

It is quite natural and human for oppressed people, or people who feel oppressed, to blame everything on the colonising power. They come to believe that if they could only gain their independence, all their problems would be automatically solved. And then, one day, they become independent and find to their dismay that their problems are not solved; on the contrary, they multiply rapidly.

The second sad result of strong anti-colonialist feelings is the behaviour it calls forth among so-called Progressive European Intellectuals. I met these P.E.I.'s all over Asia and, to put it mildly, I could not see eye to eye with them. They suffer from the modern disease of Asia-mania. For them everything Asian is wonderful and everything European is wrong. They believe that any argument between a European and an Asian can be settled before it has even started, on the simple, basic principle that the Asian is always right and the European always wrong. They keep telling their Asian friends that we, Europeans, have to approach them with great humility; that we have everything to learn in Asia and nothing to teach; that we are all criminals, exploiters and colonisers.

I personally have never approached any human being, let alone a race, to say nothing of a vast continent containing the majority of mankind, with a feeling of superiority. I just do not believe that I am really superior to any of the five Continents. Indeed, I have always hated any position of superiority or outlook and have always done my best to wriggle out of it; I have refused to employ a secretary even in an hour of dire need, simply because I could not bear to be anybody's boss. But I have not much humility either.

This may be my misfortune but where am I to acquire humility if I do not possess any? Perhaps it is this regrettable lack of humility which prevents me from feeling that I am a criminal. Europeans certainly brought a great deal of good to Asia – maybe incidentally and not out of the goodness of their hearts but even this is debatable, and then, a great deal of Asia's misery derives from Asians themselves. No, on thorough and conscientious reflection, I plead *not guilty*. My crimes may be great and manifold; but I have honestly never colonised anyone in my life.

Soon enough, of course, I noticed that the Progressive European Intellectuals do not wallow in dirt because they really feel guilty but simply because they love wallowing in dirt. There are few things they cherish quite so much as a good guilt complex. It is their greatest comfort in life.

Another idea behind this attitude is that the deeper you wallow in dirt, the more the Asians will respect you. This is a mistaken assumption. The louder and oftener you proclaim your faults, the more likely you are to convince your audience that they are indeed all you allege.

* * *

The longer you ponder over the problem, the more clearly does it emerge that colonisation has very little to do with continents and with people's colour. The 'colonising complex' is as old as the Oedipus complex; it is simply the desire to rule and exploit other people, quite irrespective of where they live and what they look like. If history teaches any lesson, it is this: revolt against oppression, whether successful or not, leads to new oppression; and defeat of an old ruling class leads to the establishment of a new ruling class rarely less cruel but often more hungry and less experienced than the old. People fight not to abolish oppression, but to make *you* stop oppressing *them*; they feel it is high time that *they* started oppressing *you*. This is reasonable enough. It is better to oppress than be oppressed. And the system also appeals to the Englishman's inborn instinct of 'taking one's turn'.

Whenever the upper dog has a chance of exploiting others, he goes ahead and exploits them, whether he is Asian or European. On the other hand, there are also those in every society who are prepared to die fighting slavery and oppression, and they are the cream of humanity.

Asia has its fair share of this cream. It has its great men and heroes. At the same time Asians are more than adept at exploiting other Asians. In fact, they had nothing at all to learn from Europeans. It was not the West that brought the caste system to India. Nor is Asia free of colour-prejudice, as many Negro visitors to certain Asian countries will rue-fully testify. But you do not even need to import Negroes into Asia to prove that point. You can observe throughout Brown Asia the snobbish respect for the lighter shades of brown. Oh, no, our Asian brethren are certainly not worse than we are; which does not mean that they are any better either.

It took the brutal defeat of the Hungarian Revolution in 1956 to bring home to many Asians the simple truth that white men may colonise other white men. I may be a coloniser as a Briton; but I am also, as a Hungarian, an erstwhile member of an oppressed nation. And if I could choose my own colonising power, I should opt for England any day instead of the Soviet Union. Ceylon, for example, was given her independence by the British freely, voluntarily and unconditionally: Hungary (or Rumania or Bulgaria) will never be given her independence by the Russians in the same way. Oh yes, I should prefer any day to be in the position of the Sinhalese who are Asians and an ex-colony to that of the Hungarians who are ex-Asians and a present-day colony.

*   *   *

Human nature, as I am sure you have noticed, is almost unfathomably complex. I have already said that we cherish a Colonising Complex in our bosoms which is simply a ferocious desire to rule and exploit, mixed with the equally ferocious desire to lead the poor, helpless, blind man across the road. To help the utterly helpless (who cannot possibly become our rivals – the baby, the blind, the dog, etc.) is just another way of displaying our virtues, proving our brilliance and reasserting our superiority.

Although I knew all this, I was nevertheless surprised at discovering a secret strong and hitherto unidentified desire deep in my heart. I noticed with growing concern that I wished to be rejected as a White Sahib. But the Asians refused to reject me because they had more sense and knew better: I was no White Sahib, only a former Hungarian refugee, more Indian or Sinhalese in some respect than the Indians and Sinhalese themselves. So I heaved a sigh and accepted my own acceptance.

I was pleased to learn that even if they had seen the budding Englishman in me, they would have felt little inclination to stab me or even to be less friendly to me. How often did I hear such remarks in India or Pakistan: 'As long as the English do not want to rule us, we have no quarrel with them at all. After all, there are no other two nations in the world who know each other better than we do.'

And then people would drag me aside, look round furtively and when convinced that no one was within hearing, whisper in my ear: 'In fact, we rather like the English.'

A strange world when it has come to that!

ETIQUETTE FOR ASIANS

A fair number of Progressive Asian Intellectuals moralise as follows: It is utterly wrong and indefensible to kick a dog in its right ribs; *consequently* it must be morally right and laudable to kick it in its left ribs.

In other words: it was wrong and unforgivable for Europeans to discriminate against Asians; *consequently* it is our natural right to discriminate against Europeans.

Of course – the Progressive Asian Intellectuals conclude – we do not deny that all human beings are equal; but we have read our Orwell and cannot help feeling that we are much more equal than they.

GLOBAL SLUMS

Every European in Asia has suddenly become extremely proud of Albert Einstein. Einstein, they proclaim sagely, was all right; he was, indeed, more than all right: he was one of the greatest geniuses mankind has ever produced. Incidentally, I had the honour and great good fortune to meet him personally and we had a few good laughs together. But 99.8 per cent of humanity (to which I belong) has only the haziest of notions as to why exactly Einstein is great. I doubt if there are a thousand people in the world who properly understand the Unified Field Theory. This being so, it is slightly ridiculous for every European in Asia to be so immensely proud of Albert Einstein's contribution to our culture. The underlying idea is, of course, that Einstein is one of our fellow-intellectuals; somewhat greater than ourselves perhaps but still of the same fibre.

Goethe again is regarded as a 'heavy and boring German' by many English people in England; for these same people, as soon as they arrive in Asia, he suddenly becomes one of the shining beacons of European civilisation. As my little seven-year-old American niece, Susan, when urged to practise her very legible but rather ugly handwriting told her mother, 'Letters are there to be read, not to be admired.'

Similarly, great artists are there to be enjoyed and understood, not to be flaunted in support of one's own self-esteem
– least of all by people who do not really care twopence
about them.

It is not so much the few great artists as the many minor
ones that make a period of art really outstanding; and in
modern times it is the *readers* and the *connoisseurs* who cause
a civilisation to flourish at a given place and period. An
Asian who truly appreciates and loves Picasso is nearer to
him than a European who in Europe sees only the Communist propagandist in him but in Asia boasts on account
of his white – although not too white – skin. An artist does
not belong to a village, or a nation, or even a continent; he
belongs to all who care for his art.

There is, however, another aspect to this. Asians also love
boasting about their own civilisation. They have exactly as
much justification in so doing as we. Not more and not less.
China, we are often reminded, had for long been a highly
civilised land at a time when savage tribes were still roaming
the marshes of Britain. That is true. But that was a long
time ago.

Asia may have been ahead of us a few thousand years
ago; it may overtake us again in the future. But it has been
left behind in the present. It is no good speaking of 'purely
technical' advances. The difference between living in a flat
in England or Holland with running hot water, central
heating and having a car, and living on a dunghill somewhere in the backwaters of India is not a 'purely technical'
difference. Nor is the sputnik or the radio-telescope a 'purely
technical' advance.

The Asians are not trying to develop the culture and
heritage peculiarly theirs and trying to prove its superiority
to ours; they are simply trying to catch up with us on our
own pitch. They are trying to industrialise Asia, to develop
commerce and communications. Their leaders do not

encourage the abstract and, no doubt, superior virtues of
the hermit. How delighted they would be to see an industrial
revolution – with all its attendant evils thrown in. They
condemn us and study us; they despise us and copy us. We
are their bogies and their ideals at one and the same time.

They are in danger of succeeding in their self-appointed
task. The philosophical contentment of the Asian is slowly
giving way to the spirit of business rivalry; their majestic
individuality to a desire to keep up with the Ching-Fungs;
their faith in the Eternal and Unchangeable is being replaced
by a burning impatience for rapid change. Confucius is
their own; their miraculous architecture is their own; but
Asian nationalism itself is an import-article from Europe.

*   *   *

It is a favourite habit of shallow minds to contrast the
admirable, intelligent and lovable man in the street with
the wicked, self-seeking and stupid politician. This is either
crass stupidity or an idiotic and irresponsible pose. The so-
called 'masses' are neither wonderful, nor intelligent, nor
lovable – they are like the rest of us, including the politicians.
We ourselves constitute the masses. All democracies have
the governments they deserve. If people elect, by their own,
free choice, stupid or self-seeking fellows to guide their vital
affairs then they must indeed be considerably more stupid
than those elected. The rulers, at least, will get the pleasure
of ruling; the masses only get the pleasure of being kicked
about by fools; while it is supposed that there are thousands
of brilliant and admirable men in their own ranks who
would make so much better Prime Ministers, Chancellors
of the Exchequer and Postmasters-General but who prefer,
because of their modesty and retiring disposition, to remain
postmen, antique dealers and solicitors' clerks.

This means not that all is well but that the politicians'
failure is our own failure. Who among us has pointed out

the undeniably right path for the world or at least the Free World to follow so far ignored by wicked and obstinate politicians? At the moment we are afraid of being blown to pieces together with our own beloved planet. Consequently we spend the great bulk of our national incomes on armaments, conventional and unconventional. We live a life much duller than that we could afford were it not for the gigantic, almost incredible, fortunes spent on armaments and at the same time our most ardent hope is that all this tremendous expenditure will remain a sheer waste of money. Our dearest wish is that our most expensive armaments will rust away, unused.

Few people care for slum-clearance and those who do think about it (I am not forgetting American aid) are inclined to think in political terms. I am not speaking of English, French, German, Greek and American slums; I am speaking of global slums which are mostly in Asia.

The Social Democratic parties of the world still think of their own people (which is right) and no one else (which is fatally wrong). Many English workmen are worse Blimps than English colonels have ever dared to be: not only do they shrug their shoulders and go their way unconcerned about foreign workers but do their level best to prevent them even from improving their own lot (remember Italian and Hungarian miners, West Indians, etc.). The Conservatives, at least, are making an effort to appear good Socialists; the Labour Party does not even care any more what it looks like. The meek acceptance of the tyranny of often selfish and short-sighted trade unions is slowly becoming the substitute for Socialism in England.

In the meantime the global slums not only grow and multiply but also come nearer and ever nearer to us – threatening the European ruling classes, whether the individual members of these ruling classes are company directors or skilled electricians. There they are, the global slum-

dwellers, ready to push on, ready to buy ball-point pens
and eventually motor cars by the million. Old-fashioned
missionaries largely failed to convert the non-European
masses to Christianity; modern missionaries, called sales-
men, would have a much better chance of converting them
to refrigerators and motor scooters. The difficulties involved
are enormous, but nothing, or almost nothing, is being done
for these global slum-dwellers. On we go manufacturing
missiles and radar equipment for a gigantic, shining, metal
refuse-dump. The world has shrunk a great deal and goes
on shrinking rapidly. The faraway global slums of yesterday
will arrive tomorrow at our own suburbs; and the day after
tomorrow their stench will reach our own, delicate nostrils.

FROM SIKLOS TO TOKYO

I was born in Siklos, Hungary.

Siklos is a small, sleepy and dusty village but for the first
ten years of my life it was for me a magnificent place and
the hub of intellectual life. After all, Siklos had 3,000
inhabitants – a veritable metropolis compared with, say, the
neighbouring Kisharsany with its few hundred souls; Siklos
was the so-called 'chief locality' of a district, with various
government offices, a tax office, a district court, two hotels
and even a bank; and we had policemen, not gendarmes –
the truest token of urbanity and adulthood. And then,
Siklos people were so immensely superior. It is hard to tell
which they despised the more, the peasants of the surrounding villages or the inhabitants of Pecs, a largish town nearby.
It was ridiculous and backward to be a villager; and it was
effeminate and smug to be a town-dweller. Siklos was just
right. Mind you, it was not enough to come and settle in
Siklos; you had to be a native of the place. Although there
was one slight blot on my ancestry as my mother had only

married into Siklos society – she had come from Budapest –
I still passed muster since even my paternal great-grand-
father had been born in Siklos. I belonged, in fact, to the
salt of the earth.

I did not know then that the people of the surrounding
villages as well as the people of Pecs thought just as poorly
of us as we thought of them. My pride in Siklos and my
local patriotism were boundless. Our local football-team
fought violent battles with those from the neighbouring
localities, especially Darda – another Siklos, not far away.
The most renowned player of our team was a barber called
Czinna. He came every day to shave my father and my
father grew much in my estimation because he was shaved
by such an eminent person. I do not think that I have
experienced a greater access of passion, a deeper emotional
upheaval than I did at the Siklos-Darda football matches.
And I do not remember many occasions in my life when I
have been more downcast than on that dark day when
Siklos was defeated by Darda, three goals to one.

When I was about four we had to move to Pecs. This was
in World War I and the army unit in which my father served
was quartered at Pecs. I was never converted to Pecs. I kept
a stiff upper lip, I endured the comforts and blessings of an
easier and better life; I tried not to show my contempt for
the city dwellers – too effeminate and smug, if you asked
me – and I remained a true Siklos boy at heart.

At the end of the war Siklos (we had returned by that
time) was occupied by Yugoslav troops and the place was
about to be incorporated in the newly born state of Yugoslavia. At school we were taught that the Serbian who had
touched off the war by killing the Crown Prince of the
Austro-Hungarian Empire was a true hero and Hungary
had been on the wrong side, while Serbia had been on the
right. Then Siklos was given back to Hungary and we were
told that the Serbian who had killed the Crown Prince was

a base assassin and that Hungary was right in every respect, while Yugoslavia – and everybody, for that matter, with the single exception of Hungary – was wrong. Naturally, I instinctively sympathised with Hungary and became a staunch irredentist at the age of six or so.

Later in Budapest, to which city we moved after the death of my father when I was ten, some subversive older friends assured me that irredentism was wrong; that Hungary had been guilty in her treatment of her national minorities, the Rumanians, Slovaks and Croats; and that the Treaty of Trianon served her right. (When I began to think for myself, I realised that Hungary had indeed behaved badly to her minorities, yet, I remained convinced that the Treaty of Trianon was stupid, unjust and vindictive.)

In the meantime, I graduated from the village to the capital and here the swing in my feelings was violent indeed. I came to adore Budapest and, in a mild way, I am ashamed of my village origin to this day. I love cities and dislike the countryside; I prefer trolley buses to daffodils and petrol fumes to the scent of acacias. Why? Simply to prove to the world and myself that I am a true metropolitan and not a little village boy.

Having left my village, I went on to leave my country, too. First it was a temporary absence, a journalistic job to be done in London, but later it became clear that this temporary arrangement was to last all my life. Suddenly I found myself a foreigner: a stranger who stuttered in a peculiar semi-Asiatic tongue, who wore too long an overcoat, clicked his heels and bowed and when asked, 'How d'you do?' explained in detail how he was. The English laughed at me. But in my eyes London and Britain, with all their pride and self-assurance and conviction that they were the finest place on earth, were only a gigantic Siklos and so I, too, laughed at them.

Here in London I also discovered that I was a white man.

I had never realised that before. Once, during World War II, I invited a Negro friend to supper. He nearly wept. He told me that while people were often kind to him, I was the first white man to invite him into his home. It was most embarrassing. I did not mean it that way. I told him that being a Central European I was not all that white. I had my darkish spots in the eyes of the real master-race. But he went on shedding his tears of gratitude. However, the one who never turned up for supper and never bothered to explain or apologise, before or since, was my grateful Negro friend.

It was in New York, after the war, that I first discovered that I was a European, too. There I learned to love Europe; I found I belonged to Europe; I was even perhaps proud of good old Europe. There is no place in the world where you can feel a better and prouder European than in the United States of America.

Having been a proud villager of Siklos, a Hungarian patriot, a lover of Budapest, a lover of London, a British patriot, a foreigner, a white man and a European, I set out on my journey to Asia. There my mind was invaded by a vague notion that I was really only a member of the human race. I am still not quite sure of this; things are not quite as simple as plausible slogans and catchwords would have us believe. But this may well be the truth. Now, as we are about to celebrate the centenary of Darwin's *Origin of Species* on the one hand, and make effective preparations to blow up our planet on the other, we may be slowly driven to the conclusion that the difference between white, brown and black men is more accidental, more environmental and much slighter than the difference between, say, cocker spaniels and Irish water spaniels; and also that there are, after all, more things to unite than to divide humanity. This, however, sounds a little far-fetched at present.

Nevertheless, my acquaintance with Asia reaffirmed the two main lessons of my younger days:

1. I often thought of my Negro friend and was often reminded of the moral I had learnt through him, namely that while he always deserves our sympathy, THE VICTIM IS NOT ALWAYS RIGHT.

2. And seeing the pride and self-assurance of countries and peoples, their conviction that they had just the right amount of sagacity, experience and intelligence as well as the happiest mixture of Western technical skill and Oriental wisdom, that they were all Chosen People with a glorious past and even more glorious future in store for them; in short, when I realised that they all regarded themselves as the Salt of the Earth, I realised that THE WHOLE WORLD IS ONE ENORMOUS SIKLOS.

JAPAN

THE FIRST MYSTERY

When I landed at Haneda airport, near Tokyo, in the company of some seventy other writers of various nationalities who had all come to take part in the International PEN Club Congress, I was stopped on the tarmac by a Japanese reporter.

'What are your impressions of Japan?' he asked me in hesitant but intelligible English and held notebook and pencil in readiness to jot down my reply.

As we had to wait for the customs anyway, I summed up my impressions of my first three minutes on Japanese soil in a concise little talk lasting about a quarter of an hour.

I finished my discourse and the reporter bowed to me: I bowed in return. When he had departed, I turned to an old Japanese friend of mine whom I shall call Tanaka. He had spent years in England and was now meeting me at the airport.

'I hope he won't take it all seriously.'

'He would take it very seriously,' Tanaka replied. 'But

you needn't worry. The man didn't understand a word you said. He doesn't speak English.'

'But he spoke to me . . .' I protested.

'He knows a few odd words but he doesn't understand it at all,' Tanaka repeated firmly. 'Apparently the office couldn't spare a man who really knows English.'

'I see,' I nodded. 'This one was just getting in some practice.'

Tanaka shook his head sadly:

'Oh no, it's not that at all. They certainly would not do a discourteous thing like that. They are really very keen to know what your impressions of Japan are.'

'They are keen?' I asked him, reflectively.

'Very keen indeed,' said Tanaka earnestly.

I shrugged my shoulders. Well, I was in the mysterious Orient.

STUDY GROUP

Tokyo was – apart from refuelling stops – the first city I saw in the Far East. My first, somewhat disappointing impression was that the Orient was not oriental enough. True, wherever you look you see notices, shop signs and advertisements in the fascinating and picturesque Japanese writing, reminding you constantly that you are not in Regent Street; it is also true that the serious, intelligent but strange faces of the men and the lovely and perhaps not quite so strange faces of the women are constant reminders that you are far east of Middlesex, and even of Budapest. Still, you heave a sigh: this would not be a bad décor for a Japanese stage show but it is not nearly Japanese enough to be real. The whole city, with its huge office buildings, noisy traffic and dazzling neon-lights might almost be taken for Manchester or Salt Lake City by one who had never been in Tokyo, Manchester, or Salt Lake City. You may see here and there a few women – and even a few men – wearing the kimono and you nod approval. But these obliging few are almost completely lost in the vast sea of the Marks-and-Spencerised crowd, all wearing mass-produced Western style suits and dresses. You know you are being silly; but, after all, you have travelled far enough and you want oriental romance and mystery for your money, however progressive you feel a modern Asian country should be. That is why I exclaimed aloud with joy when, on my journey from Haneda airport to Frank Lloyd Wright's practical joke, called the Imperial Hotel, I saw my first Japanese cinema queue. The cinema itself was of the type you may easily find in Nevada or Yorkshire. The queue too was an orderly one but, I noticed with delight, most people were not standing in the queue but squatting in it. As soon as I reached my hotel room I had a shot at squatting myself to see what it felt like. After two minutes I collapsed from exhaustion and pain. But the Japanese rest that way – the lazier types for hours on end. I have read somewhere that certain East Africans are in the habit of resting standing on one leg. A queue of people standing on one leg could not seem more grotesque to the European eye than a queue squatting patiently and happily.

'How to go Western?' has been modern Japan's main problem. They have solved it pretty quickly, I thought. They have learnt in a hundred years what had taken us a thousand to find out for ourselves. They are the biggest industrial nation in Asia. They make as good (some say better and certainly cheaper) cameras, binoculars, watches, textiles and many other things as any nation in Europe. They are 'imitative' I know. But the art of imitation and the choice of the right things to imitate require a good deal of intelligence, even brilliance. I remembered a sentence I had read in an article by Melvin Lasky, years before: '. . . perhaps superior imitation is . . . a better thing than poor first-come originality.'

To learn so much so quickly required endless concentration. The Japanese have acquired the habit of concentration: they are always on the alert and always ready to learn a little more. They will listen to a lecture with intense concentration and without raising an eyebrow for four and a half hours on end. There was a letter awaiting my arrival at the hotel, from some students who knew the names of the PEN Congress delegates and who, I thought, had sent similar letters to all those from abroad. It began: 'My dear Grandfather', which surprised me a little and went on to ask me to be so kind as to answer the following questions: What were my impressions of Japan? What is literature? What were the most pressing problems of English literature just now? How did I see the immediate future of Japanese literature? What were my views on the last hundred years of English, American and Japanese humorous writing? And so on – fifty-two questions all told.

On my first evening in Tokyo Tanaka took me for a long walk. At one point in a slum quarter we saw a large crowd squatting round something on a bombed site. There were about two hundred people, watching something in solemn, fearful silence.

Tanaka explained they were watching television. Japan, it appears, has one state-owned and three commercial television companies. The latter had drawn the logical conclusions of their existence: in a poor country like Japan it was not enough to provide programmes and pepper them with advertisements: they also had to provide free sets for people to see their advertisements. Hence this set (and many others) in the open and hence the solemn, silent and awe-struck crowd. When I got near enough to see the programme, I found that the crowd was watching *I Love Lucy*.

On we moved to the Ginza, where dozens of young men were playing on pin tables with studious but expressionless faces and with immense concentration. I found out later

that they watch Kabuki plays and *besu-boru* in the same way.
(*Besu-boru* is Japan's national sport. In America it is known
as baseball.)

By now I was feeling a little tired after my long journey
and slightly bored by the solemn and studious young men
so I suggested to Tanaka that we should go and see a *starup*
– one of Tokyo's famous strip-tease shows. We went to the
district called Shinju-ko – an ocean of amusement arcades,
restaurants, brothels and night-clubs. The place we landed
in had a night-club on street-level, and a pawn-shop on the
first floor – a most convenient arrangement. The show was
exactly what I had expected. The girls who undressed and
danced in the nude were numerous and very lovely. Just
the right entertainment for the weary traveller, I thought,
as I settled down. Then suddenly my blood chilled.

I had suddenly become aware of the intent, studious and
serious faces of young men around me. They viewed those
legs and bosoms as European university students watch a
post-mortem. One of them was even making notes.

'Let's get out of here,' I said to Tanaka, got up, and fled.

We went back to my hotel where one of Tanaka's friends
was introduced to me.

'What are your impressions of Japan?' he asked me at
once.

'Wonderful country, excellent people,' I replied. 'But, I
have a vague feeling that you don't possess much sense of
humour.'

'Not much sense of humour?' he asked me anxiously.

'No,' I shook my head. 'Some maybe. But not much.'

He reflected upon my grim and unkind statement for a
short while, I wondered if he would commit *hara-kiri*. Then
he took a little book out of his pocket and wrote something
in it. I felt absolutely certain that he was making a note for
next day – say – between eleven and eleven-thirty a.m.:
'Develop sense of humour'.

MANNERS

Before your first hour in Japan is over you will have realised that you are among exquisitely well-mannered people. It is not a veneer: it is intrinsic and inbred in a people who take all their moral obligations seriously and who live on an overcrowded island. When you have as little space to yourself as the average Japanese, you must respect other people's privacy. Take for example the public telephone in the street. It is simply placed on some street-vendor's counter – no booth or kiosk – and any passer-by could listen in to your most intimate conversations. But no one does. A man's telephone receiver is his castle.

And also within the first hour you will notice that people keep bowing to you. So you keep bowing to them. But you bow too deeply or not deeply enough; you bow to the wrong man at the wrong time; you do not clasp your hands in front of you which is bad; or you do, which is worse. Then you notice that every greengrocer's shop-girl bows with more grace and poise than any lady-in-waiting in a European court. Later still, you discover that the Japanese have a complicated hierarchy in bowing which you may try to understand but in vain. Who bows to whom? The basic rules inside the family are these: 'The wife bows to the husband' (writes Ruth Benedict in *The Chrysanthemum and the Sword* [1]), 'the child bows to his father, younger brothers to elder brothers, the sister bows to all brothers of whatever age.'

There are many kinds of bow. If you are sitting on the floor, Japanese fashion, you lean forward and touch the ground with your forehead; or else you nod. There are many intermediate varieties between these two. When bowing you must watch the other fellow from the corner of your eye, and

[1] Secker and Warburg, London, 1947

remain in a bowing position as long as he does. You must not rise before him; he will not rise before you. Inexperienced bowers stay in a bent position for hours. In the old days it was a habit of the Japanese to bow after every few words. The days of those exaggerated formalities are over. Nowadays it is quite sufficient to bow at the end of each sentence, that is, at every full stop: a nod is enough at semi-colons.

In bygone days, too, when you were riding in a vehicle and met a man to whom respect was due – which means anyone at all – you were expected to get out of the vehicle and bow to him. Today it is not absolutely essential to stop your taxi and bow to all your acquaintances, but it is advisable to do it every now and then to show that you have some manners. About a dozen times during a journey should be ample.

Here are a few more elementary rules of Japanese etiquette. Nothing too advanced, only those absolutely essential ones which may help to prevent a European from seeming rude or making a fool of himself.

On leaving the Japanese house in which you are staying you always have to declare, '*Itte mairimasu*' (I am going now), and on returning say, '*Tadaima*' (I am just back). To say on arrival that you are just leaving or on leaving that you have just come back is considered misleading.

If you are invited into a Japanese home (as you are likely to be because the Japanese are hospitable people, interested in you), take off your shoes before stepping on the *tatami* or floor mat. You will find two kinds of doors in a Japanese house; both are sliding doors. Whenever you open or close a sliding door you have to kneel down. Having spent a good deal of time on your knees, you may sit down on the floor. (The almost complete absence of furniture in Japanese houses is a brilliant idea: space may be much better utilised, and furnishing is incomparably simpler and cheaper if it does not involve buying any furniture.) You sit on the floor,

or rather, on your own legs, you are allowed a cushion, and
your body should lean forward. A man's hands should be
placed on his thighs; a woman's clasped in front of her. A
man's hands must never be placed on a woman's thighs.
Should anyone enter the room, you remove yourself from
the cushion on to the *tatami*. When the introductions are
over, you move back on to the cushion.

Now it may happen that you want to pass in front of a
sitting person. Do not hesitate, it is perfectly simple. All you
have to remember is that you must remain on your knees,
crawl along and drag both your knees behind you at
the same time. Anyone who moves his knees separately is
regarded as a lout, fit only for the pigsty.

Then tea will be served. It is very bad manners not to
sip it noisily. It shows a lack of appreciation. If a Japanese
child sips his tea (or soup) quietly, he is told off by his
mother. If you are offered more biscuits than you can
encompass, you refuse by saying that you have had enough.
Then your hostess will wrap them up for you and you take
them home. On departing you leave the slippers you had
to put on when entering the house at the door, facing
inwards, ready for the next visitor to step into.

The giving and the receiving of gifts have – as everyone
knows – their strict rules. The choice of wrapping paper for
gifts is of the utmost importance. These rules are a little
complicated and it is quite enough if the foreign visitor gets
acquainted with *dashi, hosho, torinoko, sugiwaragami, nishinouchi,
noriire, minogami* and *hanshi*. But these are the bare minimum.
The method of wrapping is also of decisive importance. I
quote from *Japanese Etiquette; An Introduction*:[1] 'Wrinkling
must be avoided and the folding should be precise. Ordinarily
the paper is wrapped so that the last fold comes on top of

---

[1] *Japanese Etiquette: An Introduction*, by the World Fellowship Com-
mittee of the Y.M.C.A. Tokyo.

the package at the right-hand edge with the end of the
paper extending all the way to the left-hand edge of the
package. For unhappy occasions, however, the wrapping is
reversed, with the last fold on the top of the package at the
left-hand edge and the end of the paper extending all the
way to the right-hand edge of the package. One must be
very careful about how the paper is folded for people are
very sensitive about it . . . Gifts with a red-and-white cord
should be tied so that the red cord is on the right; and when
using the gold-and-silver cord, the gold should be on the
right.'

At this point, I must admit, I interrupted my studies and
decided to remain a lout, fit only for the pigsty.

SAMURAI AND POSTMEN

Once upon a time I came to live in certain islands, called
the British Isles, which lie off the shores of a great continent.
When I went to explore certain other islands, called Japan,
off the shores of another great continent, I was curious to
see whether there was any similarity between the two
peoples. One had heard so much of the 'Prussians of the
East' that one wanted to find out a little about the 'British
of the East' (before settling down to study the Japanese of
the East). There must be some similarities between the
Japanese and the British, I thought; after all, environment
must have had some effect. And indeed, we do not have far
to seek. Certain parallels are so obvious that we need not
dwell upon them. Both nations are maritime nations, with
long traditions and intimate ties with the sea, both are the
most highly industrialised countries of their respective continents and both hit upon the obvious idea (obvious to sailors)
of founding an empire and trying to rule the world. Both
peoples have excellent manners, are disciplined in their own,

different ways and are able to think in global terms and in centuries – an attitude quite alien to the land animals.

I have found, I think, the point where the Japanese differ most from the English; and also the point where they almost improve on them, where the Japanese are more English than the English.

I was first of all put out to find that the 'Oriental imperturbability' of the Japanese is an illusion and a myth. They are imperturbable enough as long as they are not properly roused. But when roused they are able to fly into the most spectacular rages and the consequences are unpredictable. I have collected countless examples of what ought to be called 'Oriental perturbability'. It can be shattering enough even on the domestic scale. An English friend of mine, a bachelor, once asked his Japanese housekeeper to fetch some salt. This seemingly trivial request set off a terrific explosion. The girl wept and lamented vociferously for an hour and a half, her complaint being that by asking for the salt, her employer had been rude enough to point out that she had forgotten it. At the climax of her paroxysm she stormed out of the house, still in a state of uncontrollable fury. Two hours later she returned as calm as an angel and courteous as a geisha. The whole matter would never have been mentioned again had not my friend, five months later, been foolish enough to ask where his shoes were as he could not find them.

One of Japan's great literary works is *The Forty-Seven Ronins*, a tenth-century novel of romantic love and adventure. The story has been read by millions throughout the ages, it has been turned into a Kabuki play and is being made into a film. A retainer at the Imperial Court, anxious to humiliate a rival, advises the latter to wear the wrong pair of trousers for a ceremonial occasion. The warrior's humiliation is unutterable: and it demands a terrible vengeance. The story itself is really the history of this

vengeance – the story of forty-seven brave avenging *samurai*.
All forty-seven are killed before this terrible tale is con-
cluded; villages are burnt and pillaged; countless people
ambushed, tortured, massacred; wives sell themselves to
brothels to enable their husbands to carry on the fight etc.,
etc. It is all very admirable and heroic. And it is all because
of the wrong pair of trousers. On a similar occasion in tenth-
century Britain, when Sir Adalbert was similarly maliciously
advised in the matter of trousers and deeply humiliated
when he appeared unfittingly attired at King Edred's Court,
he simply went home and changed his trousers. And thus we
were deprived of an early masterpiece of English literature.

The point where the Japanese outdo the English in
Englishness with flying colours, is in the muddle of their
streets or rather their postal addresses. London has achieved
great and glorious results in these fields (see, if you can be
bothered, *How to be an Alien*, by the same author); yet,
London is simply nowhere compared with Tokyo. Giving
silly names to streets, roads, gardens, crescents, mews, walks,
alleys, etc. and allocating numbers to houses in a haphazard
and whimsical manner is quite a good line but it is rather
amateurish. It falls miles below Japanese standards. The
Japanese have hit upon the simple and logical idea that if
you really want muddle and chaos in your towns you must
give no names at all to your streets and no numbers to
your houses; and if you do occasionally provide names and
numbers, it should be done only to give a false lead and
increase the muddle. A postman may have a letter for, say,
Shinkichi Vyeda San (*San* stands for Mr, Mrs *and* Miss,
which is helpful for the postman); people in the neighbourhood may or may not have heard of him or her; they may
or may not be able to tell the postman whether Vyeda San
is a boy of four or a lady of eighty-seven; they may even be
able to tell the postman where Mr Vyeda – if he is a Mr –
lives and eventually the postman may or may not find him;

and Mr Vyeda himself may, if found, come in to an unclaimed inheritance of 124 million yen. Or again, he may not.

Nervous breakdown is a regular occupational disease of Japanese postmen after four years of service. There is a special hospital for nervous disorders which is reserved for postmen only, where scores of people amble about with envelopes in their hands, a vacant look in their eyes. Their lips hardly moving, they mumble addresses like '*Shibuya ku . . . Shibuya-ku . . .*' until the day when death relieves them.

DRIVING

As soon as the Japanese become motorised, they discard the last vestiges of their admirable self-discipline, oriental imperturbability – such as it is – and good manners. Not that they are alone in this: the steering wheel of a motor car has the same effect on modern civilised man as the smell of blood has on the average tiger.

But Japan, even so, has a special place among the drivers of the world. Compared with the Japanese the French are meek, cowardly and patient, the Italians polite, quiet and restrained. Siam is the only place which belongs to the same school of driving. As an official of the British Embassy in Bangkok (it could easily have been Tokyo) told me: 'Back in England on leave, and on my very first day, too, I performed a perfectly decent – nay, courteous – piece of East-Asian driving. I was fined ten guineas with three guineas costs and my licence was endorsed.'

Rush hour traffic in Tokyo has to be seen to be believed. What they do not do in the way of cutting in, crazy cornering, acrobatic overtaking, and unindicated changes of direction is not worth doing. With this type of driving one would not survive two miles even in Rome simply because no one would be expecting such feats: but in Tokyo every car driver is permanently expected to drive like a champion of the racing tracks.

The European visitor would be rather worried about the other traffic during a Tokyo taxi-ride but for the fact that he keeps bouncing wildly about on his seat and banging his head against the roof of the taxi all the time. So he is not concerned about the traffic; he is concerned about his own survival.

One day I met a taxi-driver who, to my delight, spoke not only fluent but even intelligible English. I asked him how long he had been a taxi-driver. 'Two years,' he informed me. He went on to tell me that he had been a suicide torpedo-pilot during the war. Then he added:

'I wish I could go back to my old job.'

'Why?' I asked him eagerly, hoping to discover something about the latent militaristic impulses of the Japanese psyche.

'I am a married man, sir, with four children,' he replied. 'This present job of mine is a bit dangerous, you know.'

AMUSING DEATHS

A little later I discovered that the Japanese do, in fact, laugh heartily at times. We had gone one evening to Chinzan So, which must be one of the most beautiful landscape gardens in the world, and I became involved in a long and interesting conversation with a young university lecturer. During the course of our conversation he told me something about his childhood and related how he, a country boy, had come to live in the capital.

'It was really all due to a little incident,' he smiled.

'When I was about four, the house we lived in in Tsuruoka caught fire,' he continued with a widening grin.

He seemed to be more and more amused: suddenly he burst out laughing:

'It was burnt to the ground.'

I started laughing myself.

'My father was burnt to death,' he added with a roar.

He could hardly go on. Uncontrollable mirth seemed almost to choke him. At last he was able to utter a few more words:

'And so was my mother.'

We laughed till we cried. The death of his mother was the climax of this amusing tale, nothing funny happened after that.

It is not hard to see, of course, that your Japanese friends laugh from embarrassment and not in merriment. Still, a scene such as that just described has a spine-chilling effect on you the first time you come across it. But it is, after all, just a habit, a social convention, no stranger than the English habit of describing such an event without any sign of emotion. It might even be more human to laugh merrily at the mass-extinction of your family than to show complete indifference to it.

More often than not such laughter, due to acute embarrassment, is connected with what the Japanese call 'face'. On other occasions, however, the embarrassment is unconnected with laughter and then it is more difficult to diagnose it as embarrassment. On the subject of Japanese embarrassment, the European visitor has a few essentials to learn:

1. No one will ever admit that he does not understand what you are saying. Fragments of conversation like the following are commonplace: 'Shall we eat here or go to a restaurant?' 'Oh yes.' Or: 'Which English writer do you like best?' 'Most certainly.' Or again: 'What do you think of European ballet?' 'Oh no.' The Japanese point of view is that it might embarrass you to be told that they have no idea what you are talking about. I was present at lengthy and vivacious conversations between a European and a Japanese after which the Japanese participant confessed to

me that he had had no idea what they were chatting about. The European, for his part had failed to realise that there was anything amiss in their lively exchange of ideas.

2. Generally speaking, no one will ever tell you anything that might embarrass you in any way. If you ask for pea-soup in a restaurant, the waitress will bring you dried fish instead, rather than embarrass you by asking you to repeat your order. If you ask someone in the street to direct you, he will send you miles out of your way rather than embarrass you by confessing that he has never heard of the place you are looking for, and thus making it obvious that you have chosen the wrong person for your enquiries.

3. No Japanese taxi-driver will admit that he did not understand the address you gave him and that even if he had understood it, would not know where the place is. One day I had to go from the Sankei Kaikan, the venue of the PEN Congress, to the Foreign Correspondents' Club, a journey of about ten minutes on foot. I had a notion where the Club was but not being quite sure I thought it safer to take a taxi. Before I eventually reached my destination about an hour and a half later, I had been taken to the Headquarters of the Tokyo Fire Brigade and twice to the American Presbyterian Church, eight miles outside Tokyo.

These, however, are minor matters. When something really serious happens, then they do laugh and laugh heartily.

An Englishman, long resident in Tokyo, told me this story. One day he saw a large American car turn very slowly and carefully into a narrow street where it accidentally knocked against the tricycle belonging to an ice-cream-and-cold-drinks vendor. The driver, unaware of the slight collision, drove on. The tricycle, however, was left in rather a shaky condition. Passers-by stopped and waited with interest to see whether it would collapse or not. In fifteen seconds or so it did – by that time the car had disappeared from view without anybody having taken its number. The tricycle turned over. Dozens of bottles and glasses were smashed; the street was covered with broken glass while yellow, red and green soft drinks slowly trickled towards the gutter. The little man's livelihood was trickling away with them. He surveyed his tricycle: it was badly damaged. He looked at the scene of devastation in dismay. But the people around were looking at him in even greater dismay. Would he show any unpardonable sign of despair? Would he shed tears? Would he make a scene and *embarrass* people? No, he did not. The dismay cleared from his face in a few moments. He started smiling; then he burst out laughing. The crowd started laughing, too. The laughter grew in intensity, it re-echoed through the whole district. The drink-vendor was the loudest and merriest of them all and his demeanour suggested that the whole matter hardly amounted even to a minor annoyance; this uproarious and entertaining scene more than compensated for his small loss. My friend was truly relieved. 'That's the spirit,' he said with admiration as he watched the crowd disperse and the little man walk away. Next morning my friend noticed a short paragraph in the newspaper, reporting that the cold-drinks vendor had gone home after the incident and hanged himself.

A CLUE TO THE SECRET

The random observations of one's first few days may provide a clue to a question which is always lurking at the back of one's mind. And if you tend to forget this question, a large number of the Britons and Americans you meet all over Asia – and in Europe and America, for that matter – will soon remind you of it. 'It is all very interesting,' they will say, 'what you tell me about the Japanese and their charming ways and many talents and all that sort of thing.

But I never want to see another Japanese in my life if I can help it. For me they have entirely different associations – not exactly charm and pleasantness.' This is, of course, the voice of the former prisoner-of-war and civilian internee in Japanese hands. Do not argue with them; they have very good reasons for saying all this.

What is the truth? Where shall we seek a clue to the secret?

First of all, I think, one has to remember that the Japanese are perhaps the one nation in the world who are themselves seeking a clue to a secret. They want to find the magic word opening up national success; they are searching for the Miraculous Sign-post, leading to the Right Road, for the Secret Key that opens the Gates of Wisdom and Abundance. Until the arrival of Commodore Perry they believed that Splendid Isolation was the magic phrase (what an odd, oriental idea, if one comes to think of it). Then they found a more or less satisfying answer in Industrialisation. Nevertheless, Industrialisation turned out not to be the full answer and they tried to supplement it with Fascism.

It was a peculiar, Japanese kind of Fascism: tyranny without a tyrant. Japan has always been ruled by a class or a clique, never by one single dictator. They also had a Deity – the Emperor – who was revered but not obeyed; who was prayed to like a wooden idol but was not supposed to announce his own wishes any more than a wooden idol. When in the end he did speak – and I shall describe the occasion presently – his words were obeyed with the devotion due to a miraculous happening. Indeed, he was followed with the blind devotion due to a wooden idol or to a real God.

The Magic of Fascism was wiped out simply because it did not work. It did not lead to salvation; it led to destruction and humiliation. So the other recipe – the formula of the victors, called Democracy – had to be tried. And the Japanese are still trying it.

Are they sincere in this? The question of sincerity does not come into it at all. If, when you are experimenting in a laboratory, one given mixture does not work, you try another: you substitute, say, the sulpho group for the nitro group to see whether certain results ensue. Faith and sincerity have nothing to do with it. You make your experiment and await the result perhaps with anticipation, even excitement, but always with a degree of scientific detachment.

Industrialisation did work, so the Japanese have stuck to it; should democracy work, they will stick to it, too. If not, not.

* * *

This is a possible answer to half of the question. It does not explain, however, why the Japanese soldier behaved as he did: how these instinctively courteous people – the slaves of etiquette – could behave so often with such monstrous cruelty.

To begin with, their attitude towards physical pain and suffering is different from ours. Our own stage-shows, especially when meant for children, are savage enough, still they show some kind of sophistication, if that be the right word. In a Japanese music-hall show or in a serious play you may see a man hang himself and then his corpse dangle from a tree in full view of a mildly amused audience; or a decapitated man will appear on the stage carrying his own head under his arm, and people will giggle. In one well-known play a *samurai* father warns his young son who is being operated on and is suffering excruciating pain that should he cry out or even wince, he will slay him with his sword. Such an attitude is approved of as virtuous. A young American lady told me that her Japanese dentist had treated an abscess in her mouth without an anæsthetic and made unmistakably contemptuous remarks when she made it clear that she had not enjoyed the process.

But to come back to the war; the Japanese soldier did not care for abstract notions. The Nazis were ready to die for the Fatherland; the Japanese soldier had smaller and more tangible ideals in front of him. He had to die if he lost face or honour in the village; or if he failed in his duty towards his family, his elders, his officers – and first of all towards the head of his larger family, the Emperor. He did not die for an idea; he died for a rule of etiquette.

The Japanese wants a clean name above all. He wants a clean name as keenly as the average American is supposed to want money. And a clean name means, first of all, high esteem in his family. The Japanese loves his family. He may hate every single individual member of his family – yet the love of his family will be the strongest of all his feelings.

When a Japanese soldier was captured (and not too many of them were) he gave information quite freely and without much remorse: he had lost face in any case and for him it was then all the same. England loves her dissenters and trouble-makers; here even the lunatic fringe is valued, honoured and affectionately protected. Dissension is regarded as the grain of freedom. In Japan only conformity is appreciated and tolerated. Conformity is virtue, dissension or even devia-tion is an unpardonable sin. When cruelty and inhuman behaviour to prisoners were orthodox the Japanese soldier was cruel; not because he is cruel but because he is orthodox. As soon as the Emperor told his army (this is the celebrated pronouncement of the Emperor I have referred to) that the war had been lost and that they were to lay down their arms, the army promptly laid down their arms; not a single shot was fired in defiance of the Emperor's orders. These soldiers – had the Emperor given different orders – would have been ready to die to the last man. But the Emperor had spoken and the American troops were received not with grudging acceptance of the inevitable but with curiosity, even friendli-ness. That single message of the Emperor's saved the lives of hundreds of thousands of people; and, incidentally, also saved the Emperor's throne.

When the community expected the Japanese soldier to die, he died; when the community expected him to bow his head to the conqueror, he bowed his head. When he was ordered about by a tyrannical clique he used to be a good Fascist. Now he is ordered to be a democrat and again he obeys blindly: he is a democrat. On strict orders he could even become a rebel.

WOMEN

If you want to be a Japanese, be a man. It is a man's country; and it is the women who make it a man's country.

When, after your first days in Japan, you have taken note of all the obvious and conspicuous, but none the less fascinating, eccentricities, and you try to look a little under the surface, a conviction will start growing in your mind that Japan is a country with a split personality. It is not a single split – there is a treble split, cutting in various directions and on various planes. A split was caused in this country of the invincible by Japan's defeat in 1945, the first in her history; there is another wide split between the younger and the older generation; and thirdly, between the old-fashioned and the modern woman.

These divisions are not clear cut; no division is ever clear cut; divisions are not very helpful in this respect. This confusing habit of divisions is responsible for a great deal of muddle in our world.

Some people will try to convince you that the Japanese women's liberation movement, far from being a general revolt of the younger generation is simply a revolt of the women of Tokyo and a few other large cities. The vast countryside – they say – goes on in the same old way, unperturbed. This is not true; the capital and some large cities may have been the centre of this social earthquake, but the tremors were and are being felt all over the country. It is true, however, that not all the young women are in the fight. Some of them would like to remain slaves – just as in America in the last century many Negroes fought for slavery and just as many butlers in Britain insist on voting for the Tories.

This split mind clearly manifests itself in the effect dress has on the Japanese personality. Millions of Japanese wear kimonos at home (men included, of course) and Western dress out of doors, on most but not all occasions. In Western dress the couple walk abreast, the husband is polite if not deferential to his wife and opens doors for her. But as soon as he puts his kimono on, he becomes the domestic potentate again. He walks in front of his wife; he will not dream of getting, say, a newspaper for himself, but orders his wife to fetch it for him. In the kimono he is the lord and master. And when he takes his kimono off for the family bath – in simpler households, where they have one tub only, people take their baths in turn – there is no question but that the master of the house should have the first bath.

For the old-fashioned Japanese woman, life is perpetual drudgery. Household work is heavier for her than for her European or American sister. There is less furniture in the house, it is true, but putting away the whole bed or mat every morning and bringing it out again at night is, I am told, heavier work than making the bed in European fashion. Cooking, too, means more fiddling work in antiquated kitchens and the innumerable tiny dishes they use do not turn the washing-up into a quick and pleasant pastime either. An American husband may (or must) help his wife with the washing-up; in Japan this sounds like an incredible joke, invented by anti-American slanderers. (By the way, the gulf between the patriarchal Japanese outlook and the matriarchal American outlook has been one of the most significant factors which destine these two peoples to remain strangers.)

Shopping is the only household duty which is easier for at least the middle-class Japanese woman than it is in the West. Everything is delivered to her home. Boys on bicycles keep arriving and ringing her bell twenty or thirty times every morning, each of them bringing one single item: bread, coffee, tea, rice, meat, fish, vegetables, wine, oranges, the laundry, flowers, etc. The poorer women, however, go out to do the shopping themselves. Delivery does not cost anything extra but these women dislike the idea of having to show their seedy and humble homes to tradesmen.

There is one duty of which the Japanese women are almost completely acquitted: entertainment in the home. The Japanese regard it as impolite and insufficiently formal to entertain guests at home, so they take them to restaurants and geisha-houses and the wives stay at home. (I shall have more to say later about the strong connection between the sexual and the commercial life of the Japanese.) The home is often poor and needy; the geisha-house is a place of elegance and splendour. Injustice, as always, breeds further injustice. Owing to this tradition, the Japanese man associates glamour, happiness and the beauties of life with being away from his home; he associates only poverty, drabness and worries with his wife.

It is often alleged that Japanese women do not really mind when their husbands spend nights with other women and keep up permanent connections with geishas or other ladies of easy virtue. They do mind, of course, but until recently they could do nothing about it. In most cases the men do not even bother to hide their adventures from their wives; there is no secrecy about visiting prostitutes. Divorces are few and far between (well below 20,000 a year in the whole country) nevertheless, they are possible; but the husband's adultery is not legal ground for divorce.

What about the adultery by the wife? The problem does not arise. The Japanese are proud to emphasise that their women are the most faithful in the world. This is true. The reason for this is the shining virtue of Japanese women, slightly enhanced by a complete lack of opportunity.

If the poorer woman's life is perpetual drudgery, the richer woman's life is complete boredom. They have servants who do all the chores for them and consequently they have nothing to do but go with other bored ladies to the Kabuki or watch baseball. But you cannot always go to the Kabuki or watch baseball. So they sit at home and grow fat. Not that they all grow fat; indeed, nowhere in the world have I seen so many exquisitely beautiful women as in Japan.

Even so, the old-fashioned woman is not the withering, broken flower one would imagine. She is, more often than not, a pretty formidable personality, with a great deal to say about her children's education and marriage and also about money matters. And she says what she has to say pretty distinctly. She is not only a slave in the background; she is also a tyrant in the background.

It was against this situation that the younger generation rebelled so forcefully. The Americans have liberated at least the women of Japan or have given them the chance of liberating themselves. Today, women have the vote; they study at the universities; they take jobs; fewer and fewer marriages are arranged by the parents without consulting the young people concerned (although this is still the general rule in Japan). Many women are determined fighters for equality. But fighting for equality is definitely an outdoor activity. When the brave suffragette arrives home and puts on her kimono, she will still leap to her feet and make a dash for the newspaper as soon as her husband snaps his fingers.

THE GEISHA

Europeans of both sexes seem to be under the impression that the geisha girl is a kind of superior prostitute. But most European husbands (which category, I repeat, includes Americans) on their return from Japan, are at pains to explain that the geisha girls are not prostitutes at all: nothing could be farther from the truth – they are highly cultured young ladies with exquisite manners; they are dancers, singers and entertainers of talent, and it is not on their skill in the art of love but on their wit and repartee that their reputation rests.

The truth is that the geisha girl is a cultured, charming and highly trained young prostitute with a gift for repartee. As far as the repartee is concerned, I spent one evening in the company of geishas and got much more repartee than I had bargained for. As soon as the young lady, who wore a beautiful kimono and a very elaborate hair style, discovered, after a few dozen respectful bows on her part, that I was treating her as an equal, she ceased to stand on ceremony with me and became as cheeky (though endearingly cheeky) as any spirited European schoolgirl. She pulled faces at me and dug me in the ribs, and whenever she noticed that my squatting technique did not quite come up to scratch, she would give me a push, so that I lost my balance and rolled over.

It is quite true, nevertheless, that while all geishas can be bought for the night (it is a matter of price and a very high price at that), a geisha party, much more often than not, means only supper, drinking *sake*, watching dancing and listening to singing, and gay conversation (full of repartee). '*Mamasan*' is not surprised if someone wishes to linger late in one of those tiny little Japanese houses where the parties take place, but as a rule, after midnight the guests return to their family hearths.

At the base of all this expensive and ritual entertainment lies an ancient oriental tradition, called the Expense Account. Any attempt at explaining to my readers what is meant by an Expense Account would take us too far afield. Suffice it to say that it became popular in Japan well after the Meiji Restoration, in fact, in the MacArthur era. And when I say *popular*, I am not using the word injudiciously. In no country in the world are sex-life and big business so inter-dependent as in Japan. No contract, worthy of the name, has ever been signed anywhere other than in a geisha-house. If you want to do business you have to throw a geisha party. No geisha party – no business. And that's that.

A young German who had been living in Tokyo for about four years and was on the way to making a business career for himself, talked to me on this subject:

'I am talking to you as man to man,' he said. 'Please don't give me away, it would make me ridiculous. I should lose face. Promise?'

I promised.

He looked round cautiously and then went on:

'I love my wife. She is a Japanese girl. I have never been unfaithful to her and do not intend to be. All the same, I have to spend at least three nights a week in brothels. Very well, call them geisha-houses. I call them brothels. I slip away at midnight all right as, in fact, many of my Japanese business acquaintances do, too. It's not so bad when you can slip out. But I can't get out of going to the parties. How would you like to go to brothels three times a week?'

I did not reply to this question; it seemed much too personal.

'My wife does not suspect me of being faithful to her,' he went on. 'That's my shady secret. She would think rather poorly of me if she found out. You won't talk? You promised . . .'

I told him not to worry.

'The other day I thought I had tricked three Japanese,' he said with a wide grin. 'I produced the contracts from my desk out of the blue and handed them a pen. All this was in my office, mind you. They were so taken aback and embarrassed that they signed. After they'd gone, I felt pretty elated. "No geishas for me tonight," I thought, rubbing my hands with satisfaction. But I laughed too soon. That evening, the three Japanese gentlemen, all smiles and bows, reappeared in my office. They did not explain why they had come. They didn't need to. Off we went to the bro . . . I mean to one of those houses of traditional geisha entertainment.'

★   ★   ★

The geishas are the aristocracy of an old profession. No clan, however, consists of an aristocracy only. Tokyo, I believe, has almost as many street-walkers as London. And then there are the brothels, proper and undisguised. Yoshiwara alone employs about a thousand girls in its three hundred establishments. Then there are the ON LIMIT nightclubs (meaning that they were not out of bounds to American soldiers). The hostesses in these night-clubs may be taken elsewhere if you pay the proprietor some compensation. One night four of us – a married couple and a friend of mine – ventured into an On Limit place. As soon as we sat down at a table, two hostesses appeared, bowed and sat down next to my friend and myself: as unaccompanied males we were considered free prey. I did not say anything to the very attractive young lady who attached herself to me but, after five minutes, I asked her for a dance. Considering the way I dance this was not too kind of me. As soon as we could speak in private, she asked me in slow and precise English:

'Do you desire me?' These were the first words she uttered.

I was a little embarrassed; no woman had ever opened a

conversation with me in this way before. But I have been a
polite man all my life, so I told her that I did.

She bowed deeply.

Apparently it was very kind of me to desire her.

*   *   *

The Japanese are reported to be sexually more potent and
active than any other race, except the Negroes. I do not
know whether this is true or merely self-advertisement.
Nevertheless, a certain amount of evidence goes to suggest
that this allegation has a great deal of truth in it. Yet,
Tokyo is not a sexy place; it is not erotic; it is simply
copulative.

Most people visit hotels for this purpose. All the hotels in
Tokyo – with the exception of a few international ones –
cater for this type of clientele quite openly; there is nothing
illegal about it. They have price lists for one hour, two hours,
etc. In addition, these hotels have their ordinary tourists
and permanent residents but they would not be able to live
on them alone.

'There are about 20,000 hotels in Tokyo,' a Japanese
friend explained to me. 'Say they all have at least ten rooms.
They must hire these rooms out at least five times a day to
make them pay. That means a million couples – two million
people a day. And that's only in the hotels. Not counting
the brothels at all. And all this in Tokyo alone.'

*   *   *

One night, walking with this same Japanese friend, I noticed
a young man with painted lips and false eyelashes, swaying
his hips and ogling me in a lurid way. He had a horrid
fascination for me – I had never seen anything so degraded,
a human being sunk so low before.

'Are there male geishas, too?' I asked my friend.

'Not yet,' he said. 'But the idea may have a future.'

'What about these male prostitutes?' I asked him. 'They work in exactly the same way as their female colleagues?'

'Oh no,' he shook his head. 'They'd like to. But they are much cheaper.'

*   *   *

The authorities do not like this situation. They are trying to rid Japan of the brothels and clean up the prostitution racket. The task is about as simple as the abolition of alcohol was in the United States in the 'twenties. The authorities are even prepared to distribute capital among brothel-keepers to help them to resettle themselves in some decent trade. The gentlemen concerned take the money and carry on in business. Some of them use this welcome and unearned capital to buy a few more girls. Yokohama, on the other hand, regards the whole of this legislation as outrageous. 'No self-respecting international port can be without its brothel districts' is the slogan.

The *Asahi*, one of Tokyo's daily papers, in its English edition, wrote a somewhat discouraged report on the progress of this cleansing campaign.

'The Government's campaign to encourage brothel-operators to switch to more respectable lines of business is getting nowhere fast. Brothel operators show every sign of intending to remain in business as long as possible. The few who have ostensibly changed their business are in fact continuing to operate exactly as before: their new enterprises are only a more shrewd camouflage for the business of girls for hire.

'Police Agency Director Eizo Ishii stressed the need for dealing more sternly with brothel operators, some of whom carry their contempt for the Anti-prostitution Law so far as to hire extra girls. The Agency reports that of more than 16,800 operators throughout the country, only 5.6 per cent have switched their business. Many of those who have switched, however, are carrying on their old business under the guise of inns and restaurants.

'The only noticeable change the brothel operators are making is in the names of their establishments. Changes are being made in Kinugawa, about a hundred miles north of Tokyo – the girls there have discarded their *old style* Western dress and have now got themselves up as '*geishas*'.'

And then the last, somewhat melancholy but perplexing intelligence about brothel owners: 'Some have become golf-course operators.'

CHILDREN OF THE SUN

The widest cleavage in Japan is that between the old and the young: two generations face each other with little understanding or patience. The elder people regard the post-war generation as unworthy sons of great ancestors; the young ones look on their elders as sticklers for an outmoded way of life, paragons of meaningless, empty formalities, in fact, living intellectual corpses. Young people who are now aged twenty to twenty-five received their early education under the Old Empire; then suddenly they were required to forget everything they had been taught and accept a completely new set of values. These people have the worst of two worlds. The teenagers are more or less free from such complexes, they are outspoken and frank, yet they are a generation which has lost its bearings.

What does a generation do which wishes to protest against something, but is not quite sure against what? What do people do who have a strong urge to say something to the world but do not really know what? They usually do three things: (*a*) wear Edwardian clothes or their equivalents; (*b*) discover sex as an amazing new concept, and (*c*) commit suicide.

(*a*) Japan has her Teddy-boys: they dress differently from ours but the basic ideas of the two movements are the same. They have multi-coloured shirts and jockey caps; they are called *tayozoku*, 'Children of the Sun'. (This name comes from a best-selling novel dealing with this perplexed generation.) They often behave rather objectionably, but murder and rape are still the exception: the rule is simply noise and rowdiness.

What is this idea? Why do we find Teddy-boys all over the world? One of the great troubles of our age is a shortage of good causes. Where is the fervour of the 'thirties? Where are the excitement, the devotion and red-hot partisanship that accompanied the Spanish Civil War? The hydrogen bomb may be more decisive for the fate of humanity but you cannot be for or against the Bomb. It may be against you; you cannot be against it. The world may be divided into two halves but both halves profess or pay lip service to the same ideals; peace and democracy. Where are the old days when a dictator called himself a dictator? Britain may be divided into two parties; but both stand for some sort of vague and lukewarm welfare-state socialism. There is nothing really to choose between them. On the whole, there are very few good causes left. The world is full of ardent young men, keen latter-day St Georges – and there are not enough dragons to go round.

This regrettable shortage of good causes creates frustration and neurosis on an intellectual level. On an un-intellectual level it created Teddy-boys. The Teddy-boy of England, the *tayozoku* of Japan, the *jampec* of Hungary are all champions in search of a cause, adventurers in search of adventure, crusaders in search of an *ersatz* Holy Sepulchre. Their attitude is a protest; though they do not know how and why and to whom to protest, or what about.

(*b*) Japan's young people have also discovered sex as a new gimmick. I have spoken of the sexual morality of

Japanese prostitutes which is fairly low. I have spoken of the sexual morality of the average Japanese male which is pretty low, too – not unlike ours in Europe. It is, however, much less hypocritical. The Japanese male believes – rightly or wrongly – that sex is something enjoyable. He would go so far as to say that sex is fun. He is not ashamed of his sex-life just as he is not ashamed of being drunk. But sex is on a lower plane of life and no more important than, say, smoking. Smoking, too, is all right but, like sex, it must not interfere with really essential matters. In Japan of a generation ago, sex was practised but never mentioned, never even referred to in polite circles; it was considered much more immoral to talk sex than to practise it. Today, young people not only practise it, which could perhaps be accepted as an old habit, but they speak of it quite openly, which strikes at the very root of morality.

Upper-class girls as well as farmers' and fishermen's daughters were (not without many exceptions, of course) rather easy going in the past, too. The great sexual freedom of the middle classes and especially of university students is a post-war phenomenon. '*Avant*' is the name they use for pre-marital relations.

'The Japanese girls are certainly not worse than the Europeans. But the point is that they used to be much better,' an elderly and excellent Japanese friend told me once. 'The trouble is that the average middle-class girl will give herself if she can see her action as self-sacrifice. European girls give themselves in a moment of weakness; the Japanese in a moment of strength. They simply cannot resist the temptation of sacrificing themselves. I believe that this ardent, almost hedonistic, love of self-sacrifice is the real, and as yet unidentified, clue to our national character.'

Moralists and puritans keep warning us that laxity in sexual morals brings about the downfall and the defeat of a nation. A glance at modern history seems rather to suggest the reverse process: defeat of a nation brings about sexual laxity.

(c) Suicide is also a solution. 'The number of suicides among youth . . .' (*The Times* reported from Tokyo in 1957) '. . . is twice as large as the number of deaths from tuberculosis, once the greatest single "killer" in this country – and it continues to increase.' Suicide has, of course, a great and honourable tradition in Japan as a means of cleansing one's name and purifying one's memory. 'There is a great decline in *hara-kiri*,' quite a few people informed me with nostalgic sighs. When it occurs, it is front page news but it does not occur nearly often enough. Modern suicide is different. It has no *aim*; it only has a *cause* and often enough lacks even that. People, for instance, leap off a notorious rock in Yokohama in such great numbers that the police have found it necessary to put up notices all the way to the top. The first notice you come to bids you go to the police with your troubles and assures you that you will find them sympathetic; the second reminds you of your family and of the sorrow you will cause to those who love you dearly; the third and last begs you to stop and think again. But it is of no avail.

'This is really terrible,' my elderly friend whom I quoted above remarked as we walked down from the cliff in Yokohama, 'Japan is leading the world in the number of suicides.'

'She isn't,' I replied. 'Sweden has more suicides.'

He remained silent for a moment, then continued:

'I may be a bit of an old-fashioned nationalist, you know. I stand for the old virtues and traditions. But I am not really worried about the youth of Japan. They will settle down and sober up all right. They may be perturbed today but they are not cynical. It is not only that they are breaking with tradition: they are looking for something new and worthwhile. And, you see, they have immense economic difficulties which are all-important. Most of them are

shockingly poor. We also have over-production of intellectuals; well, it may be only of graduates, but it is over-
production. There is a wealth of talent and ambition in this
country, which means that there are too many first-rate
candidates for all jobs. Do you know that there are about
2,000 candidates for the twenty Fulbright scholarships avail-
able in Japan? Yet, economic conditions are improving
rapidly and that means at least half the solution.'

We walked on in silence.

'Are you sure,' he asked me at last, 'that there are more
suicides in Sweden than here?'

'Practically certain.'

He was pained. He deplored these suicides; still, he would
have felt happier if Japan had held the world record.

BUDDHA AND MOSES

The Japanese are as religious as the English. In other words
they are not very religious and religion, indeed, plays only
a secondary part in their lives. The English are baptised in
church, they marry in church and are buried by the church,
and these three events constitute the average Englishman's
total connection with the church. Yet, England *is* a Christian
country because of a prevailing Christian tradition, much
more important perhaps than Christian dogma. Similarly,
Japan is a Shintoist country because of the prevailing
Shintoist tradition. There are Buddhist Shintoists in Japan,
Catholic Shintoists and even Shintoist Shintoists.

In one sense Shintoism is a national religion like Angli-
canism; but in another sense it is not a religion at all in our
sense of the word. It is a mixture of nationalism, ancestor-
worship, belief in the purification of the soul, a galaxy of
superstitions. 'One cannot speak of State Shinto as a Vast
Established Church, but one can at least call it a Vast

C

Establishment,' says Ruth Benedict. That is exactly why Shintoism was disestablished after the war and dragged down rather abruptly from its exalted pedestal.

I visited the famous Buddhist Temple of Asakusa Kannon. It reminds you of the big cathedrals in our modern cities: tourists mingle with worshippers, priests with fortune tellers. I had my fortune told: 'Your wishes will be fulfilled. Someone is ill in your family but he will soon recover. You are waiting for someone and he (or she) will be very late. You are on a journey now and your trip will be a success. If you get married you will be happy.' And all this for ten yen – about threepence.

Before people start to pray they clap their hands three times. In the neighbouring Shinto shrine they ring a little bell. This is to call God's attention to the prayer.

How do Western religions fare and prosper in Japan? I made two rather startling discoveries during my researches.

1. 'Christianity,' an English friend, a teacher and a lay preacher, told me, 'will never win Japan over. There is no doubt they find the teaching of Christianity interesting; they are drawn towards its philosophical mysteries. But as soon as you broach the subject of Christian morality, they cool off. They have enough worries without Christian morality. Besides, they do not like mixing their religion with morality.'

2. There is one Western religion (if you can call it Western) which has gained ground in Japan. It is Judaism. Surprising as it may sound, the number of Jewish Japanese is growing. Conversion to Jewry is not a mass movement yet but it is under way.

What is the explanation? Christianity has failed to make any great headway not only because of its morality but also because of its theory of salvation. The Japanese is always an ancestor-worshipper at heart and cannot accept the idea that while he himself could in certain circumstances be

saved, his ancestors are bound to perish because they had
no chance of embracing Christianity. The Jewish religion
takes a more lenient attitude: a good and fundamentally
decent life secures resurrection for all and sundry when the
Trumpet is blown. Former Buddhists and Shintoists may
join in the general rejoicing.

So Japan has recently acquired a fair number of Jewish
Shintoists, too. The conquest is slow, however. The time
seems yet distant when Japan will be as Jewish as Tel Aviv,
let alone New York. At present there is really not one single
district in Tokyo where you can get along with Yiddish only.

PICKLED CHRYSANTHEMUM

Japanese food is amusing; it is also beautiful to look at;
sometimes it is good to smell, and quite pleasant to listen to.
To eat – well, that is an entirely different question.

It is difficult and often pointless to criticise other people's
food. The Japanese like their diet and why shouldn't they,
if the English like theirs? *Kombu* (a kind of seaweed) is not
less delicious than boiled cabbage – although I would not
go so far as to say that it is much more delicious. But, as I
have already mentioned, Japanese food has a great many
good points.

1. Japanese food is, first of all, entertaining. *Sukiyaki*
(pronounced: skee-ahki) is great fun socially. It is prepared
from scores of ingredients and is cooked at the table in a
large, black frying pan. Its main ingredient is sliced beef and
it is the only Japanese dish which contains an appreciable
amount of meat. (The average annual meat consumption of
the Japanese is three pounds per head.) The preparation
of *sukiyaki* takes hours and it can be very amusing because –
I am told – nothing prevents people from talking extremely
wittily while waiting for their food.

Sukiyaki is a dish of Chinese origin; that is why it is really good. It was imported into Japan less than a hundred years ago and is popular with foreigners and with the young. (The split between generations runs through the menu, too. Young people prefer Chinese and Western dishes; their elders remain nationalists and traditionalists even on the chopstick level.)

2. Japan – like the United States – is a land of Beautiful Food. In America you see glamorous peaches, seductive pears, gorgeous plums and superb grapes. It is true that they all taste like raw carrots watered down but I am talking of visual beauty now and in this field they are unparalleled. Similarly, in Japan you will be served, even in the most modest *yadoya*, with flower-shaped cabbage, maple leaf-shaped carrot, and beetroot *à la* Salvador Dali; the fish will look at you from the bottom of the dish with a pearly, if somewhat reproachful, eye. And it is not only the form but also the colour schemes which will dazzle and enchant you. It would be a pity, you feel, to disturb this artistic *arrangement*. Usually, it *is* a great pity and you regret it bitterly.

3. The food often smells good; sometimes it sounds good, too. The noises a gathering of really polite Japanese produce to prove to their host that they do appreciate his efforts and generosity, amount to a Symphony of Brillat-Savarin in A major.

So the appearance, the smell and the sound of their food surpass anything to be found in France. It is the taste, and the taste only, which is open to objection. Nevertheless, the Japanese have a number of delightful dishes. Their pickles are excellent; *sushi* (small balls of rice, wrapped in seaweed and flavoured with vinegar) is a real delicacy; the octopus there is better than any I ever tasted in Hungary. (Yet, I felt that if my mother-in-law prepared octopus with a little paprika-sauce – as she invariably prepares the national dishes of all peoples – it would be better still.) If you like bamboo sprouts and pickled chrysanthemum you will find Japan a gourmets' paradise. I, personally, also love their chopsticks. I am rather clumsy with my hands but I have one real accomplishment: I can use chopsticks with the ease and assurance of an elderly *samurai*.

One day I was discussing Japanese food with an American friend of mine in the Foreign Correspondents' Club in Tokyo. He agreed with everything I had to say on the subject (all I have just repeated here) but when I finished, he started shaking his head thoughtfully:

'What gets me is the raw fish they eat,' he said. 'Don't that just show you how uncivilised they are? Raw fish! For Pete's sake, how primitive can you get?'

'You talk,' I objected, 'as if they gobbled down raw fish indiscriminately. It is only a very small part of their diet. Only a few kinds of fish are eaten raw, and only when quite fresh and . . .'

'Aw, forget it!' he interrupted me vehemently. 'You can't tell me. Only barbarians eat raw fish.'

There was a long silence. Then I asked him:

'Do you like roll-mops?'

'Sure,' he replied.

'And oysters?'

'Boy, lead me to them. My staple food.'

'And do you eat them raw or do you cook them first?'

The American eyed me:

'Pardon me; that's quite another thing.'

'Of course! For one thing, it is what *we* ourselves eat. Furthermore, we do not call it raw fish; we call it oysters.'

THE EARTH SPIDER

Naturally, I went one day to the Kabuki Theatre; a visit to Japan without seeing Kabuki is like a visit to Paris without seeing the Louvre. The Kabuki programme started at eleven o'clock in the morning with a seventh-century love-thriller involving Prince O-ama and Princess Nukada. There were three more plays in the morning; then we had an hour's break for lunch. In the afternoon it began all over again with a play called *Onna Shijin*. The hero of this was Gyo-Genki, a supremely beautiful woman and a great poetess, the daughter of Gyo-bo, a 'madman in a house of pleasure'. Quite a promising start. The play itself lived up to our expectations.

Then came my own favourite, the *Earth Spider*. When the curtain rises we see the orchestra squatting at the back of the stage (as in all Kabuki plays), amid very impressive and beautiful scenery. We see a nobleman by the name of Minamoto Yorimutsu. He has fallen ill, and cannot understand what is wrong with him. People, by the way, do not speak in Kabuki plays: they chant in an artificial, monotonous, high-pitched voice; they also moan, mutter, groan, squeal, wail, whimper, whine, snivel and roar. This is a very ancient tradition and if you start watching Kabuki plays at the age of two, you may get used to it. If you start later, you wonder.

Yorimutsu is visited by Kocho, a ravishingly beautiful lady-in-waiting, who dances for the sick man. The dance does not cure him. (It would have cured me, but that is not the point.) Kocho is followed by another visitor in the guise of a travelling priest. But he is not a travelling priest at all, far from it: he is the Earth Spider. From his mask you can see immediately that he is not a sympathetic character. He walks in extremely slowly, roughly a quarter of a mile per hour. A number of other people – Yorimutsu's servants – sit, kneel and squat about. Some people among the audience shriek with excitement. At last the visitor throws a spider at Yorimutsu who is, however, on the alert; he jumps up, snatches his sword and slashes at the sham priest. The latter, however, vanishes into thin air. 'Vanishing into thin air,' is represented by his strolling away rather slowly and comfortably.

All the members of the Yorimutsu household now gather together and decide that quick action must be taken. The Earth Spider must be sought out in his cave and killed. For about half an hour they chant and whine, 'Let's follow him! Let's run after him, we mustn't give him a chance to run away.' There is tremendous excitement, expressed by the fact that they all sit about quietly, almost motionless. They repeat: 'Let us hurry, let us gallop! We have not a moment to lose!' Whereupon they all go on sitting there.

The afternoon wears on. Suddenly Yorimutsu shouts:

'Aa . . .!' (Emphasis on the second 'a'.) He stamps his foot twice. The chorus starts chanting again!

'Go, go and avenge yourself on the Earth Spider.'

Yorimutsu gives his answer in whispers: he informs his household that he is in a frantic rage and that they must hurry desperately, otherwise the monster might get away. One cannot be quick enough in such matters. Then he declares, 'Aa!' again and stamps his feet three times.

When I wake up about three-quarters of an hour later, the chase is at its height. Three men are moving about the stage to declare about a dozen times that everything depends on speed, otherwise the monster might have a chance to escape. Then the pace of the chase quickens; the three men – still motionless – become more emphatic on this point and sit down to debate it. 'Let us not spare ourselves! Who thinks of himself in such an hour as this? We have a sacred duty to perform.'

A number of new pursuers now arrive, accompanied by a sort of gentle lullaby. They fully agree with the views of the Three. 'We cannot have a moment's rest until that curse, the Earth Spider is slain.' They sit down. A boy comes in moaning: 'Let us pursue him!' He performs a dance with two flags. After the dance the boy says: 'Let us not waste a single moment,' and dances another dance with seven fairies. The three original pursuers, still remarkably fresh although they have been squatting on the floor for so long, shout as the boy dances: 'Hurry, hurry! Not a moment is left!' The air is now so charged with urgency and tension that everyone sits down: the boy, the seven fairies and all.

Thirteen other people rush in on their knees. They lie down and kick their legs up into the air. They get up after a considerable time and dance first a doll-dance, then a puppet-dance and finally a Japanese polka. When this is over two men drag in a pedestal and leave it on the right side of the stage.

Someone starts knocking. The knocking goes on for twenty-three minutes. Another person chants: 'Ooooooh . . .' with guitar accompaniment for thirty-four minutes. Then he says: 'Ooooooh . . .' without the guitar for seventeen minutes. Then guitar without 'Ooooooh . . .' for eighteen minutes.

The cave is pushed on with the monster inside. The pursuers reappear all dressed in yellow (I forgot to mention that they all went out during the 'Ooooooohs'. One of them makes a brief (nine minutes) chanting speech on the theme, 'We must not waste a minute otherwise the monster might get away.' They all squat, then get up, go out and reappear in green. This time they tell us about the frightful and hair-raising fate that awaits the Earth Spider.

They surround the cave and look at the monster but none of them sees him. The monster utters an awful and terrifying sound: no one hears him. The pursuers say: 'We shall never find him. Our relentless pursuit was all in vain. The monster has managed to get away. Alas! All hope is now lost.'

They dance round the cave. (They are in purple now.) Even the monster cannot bear to leave them in such deep despair any longer, so he comes out of the cave. At once they all sit down. A great deal of chanting ensues; the monster prepares for the final life-and-death struggle. But no one offers combat: in fact, no one moves. Suddenly the monster, the Earth Spider, collapses and dies. I think he has had a stroke. Boredom may have brought it on.

The monster is dead. The pursuers dance round his corpse and congratulate one another on their bravery and resourcefulness.

There were two more Kabuki plays that evening. One about a mask maker, the other about a young widower who still adored his deceased wife. These two last plays, however, lacked the liveliness and raciness of the *Earth Spider*.

THE FROG AND ETERNITY

I was about nine years old when I heard a certain old joke – old even when I was nine. I thought it very funny. A man is asked whether he can play the violin. 'How should I know,' he replies, 'when I never tried it?'

I remember I was, for a long time, intrigued by the possibility that I, too, might be a violin virtuoso. I felt I ought to try, but have never done so to this day.

* * *

Many of my Japanese friends, as well as my Japanese publishers, gave me books of Japanese poetry translated into English. I had known something of Japanese poetry and its basic rules, the frequent alternation of five and seven syllables and a few other points, but now that I was reading more of them than ever before in my life, these poems really started growing on me. Soon I could not resist the temptation of trying my own hand at this art. So I wrote a poem.

> *I am looking at a frog.*
> *He smiles back at me.*

> *Frogs' smiles always remind me of*
> *Eternity.*

As this was definitely encouraging, I wrote another one after a few days' reflection:

> *I am looking at a frog.*
> *He smiles back at me.*
> *Frogs' smiles always remind me of*
> *Snow.*

And who can blame me for turning it into a trilogy?

> *A frog looks at me.*
> *I am smiling back at him.*
> *My smile always remind frogs of*
> *The Spring and the Moon.*

Ah, the Moon . . .

I showed my poems to some Japanese friends who all declared that they were superb, verging on the great. They said this so convincingly that for a while I was not at all certain who was pulling whose leg. But when my three poems were translated into Japanese and published in one of the leading poetry magazines, I became pensive and wistful.

I had known nothing of my power, simply because I had never tried to write Japanese poetry, just as I had never tried to play the violin. Is it possible – I ask my readers – is it possible that I am one of the greatest Japanese poets of this age?

FORMOSA

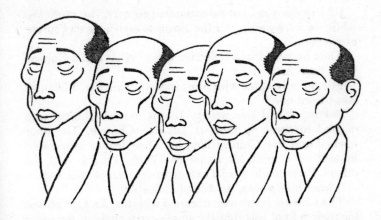

HONOUR AND PRIVILEGE

I did not go to Formosa at all. But I sensed the air of Formosa.

★ ★ ★

One day in Tokyo I was sitting in the room of a Hungarian friend of mine whom I shall call Peter. He is an altogether excellent fellow and one of the most modest men I know. Which does not mean that he is really modest; he is simply more modest than the rest of us. Certain things may happen, however, which are bound to put ideas into even the most modest heads. Something of this sort was just happening then and I am not blaming Peter at all for being tempted to put on airs.

We were sitting talking, as I have said, when the telephone rang. It was the Japanese clerk at the reception desk to inform Peter that someone wished to speak to him.

'Send him upstairs to my room,' Peter instructed him. I must add that in addition to his modesty Peter also possesses another virtue: he is completely lacking in pomposity.

'If I understood the receptionist properly,' he remarked while we were waiting for the visitor to arrive, 'it's a Chinese gentleman.'

Then he added in a reflective tone: 'What can a Chinese want from me?'

I could only agree with him: indeed, what can a Chinese want from one?

But my friend was wrong. It was not 'a' Chinese who desired to speak to him: it was five Chinese. The door opened and five Chinese filed in. Their leader introduced himself – I caught his name as Ching Tsu-lai – and the others. Peter made a brief extempore speech of welcome.

'Please take a seat,' he ended amicably.

The Chinese gentlemen declined with thanks. One reason for their refusal was that the single extra chair in the room could hardly accommodate five people; but their other, and as it seemed to me their main reason for refusing to take a seat, was that they had come on an official and formal errand and insisted on speaking to Peter standing up. They expressed themselves at great length with the oriental circumlocution and courtesy we know so well from the novels of Pearl S. Buck and which we had always thought a bit exaggerated for the sake of literary effect. The gist of Mr Ching's lengthy oration was that they had been sent by Generalissimo Chiang Kai-shek to invite Peter to Formosa in the Generalissimo's name.

'Are you sure you mean me?' asked Peter with genuine surprise. 'You mean that the Generalissimo has sent his personal invitation to *me*?'

'The Generalissimo would regard it as a major achievement of his life,' replied Mr Ching, 'and a true honour and privilege if such a leading light of Hungarian literature, such a valiant hero of the historic Hungarian revolution were to honour our unworthy island with a visit. And I should like to be permitted to add that it would be an

unforgettable red-letter day, not only for the Generalissimo
but for every man, woman and child in Formosa if you
kindly condescended to visit us.'

Peter is at the moment stateless and, as a rule, experiences
the greatest difficulty in obtaining a visa for any country at
all. It was an entirely novel experience for him to be invited
to a country by a deputation of five, the personal emissaries
of the Head of State; his arrival anywhere had never been
regarded as a red-letter day by any state, large or small,
free or subjugated. So Peter informed the delegation that
while it had not been his original intention to visit Formosa,
adding quite frankly that he had feared visa difficulties, he
could not resist this great honour and kind invitation, of
which he felt himself unworthy. So he was glad to accept it
and would like to leave for Formosa in five days.

Mr Ching was overwhelmed with delight and gratitude.
He thanked Peter, not only in his own name, not only in
the name of the whole delegation, not only in the name of the
Generalissimo but he assured Peter of the everlasting gratitude of the entire Chinese nation. They agreed to keep in
touch while the formalities were being settled and the exact
time of Peter's departure from Tokyo was being fixed and
then the five grateful Chinese gentlemen filed out of the
room.

I have told you that Peter is a modest man by nature.
No one can blame him if his ego was somewhat inflated by
these events. Chiang Kai-shek . . . a delegation of five . . .
the everlasting gratitude of the whole Chinese nation. My
foot!

I left Peter half an hour later. I saw him every day at the
Sankei Hall where the PEN Conference was taking place.
I did not count the days but after about a week it occurred
to me that the five days had passed and Peter ought to be
in Formosa. So I asked him:

'What has happened? Aren't you going to Formosa?'

'No, I'm not.' He shook his head even more modestly than usual.

'Aren't you?' I said in some surprise. 'And why not?'

'My application for a visa was refused.'

THE PHILIPPINES

ANGRY YOUNG NATION

It is only a few hours' flight from Tokyo to Manila but these few hours take you into a different world. Japan is Buddhist-Shintoist: the Philippines are Christian; Japan is an Asian nation which is trying hard to become Westernised: the Philippines have already become over-Westernised in some respects and are now trying to acquire a more Asian face; Japan is Japanese: in the Philippines you find a burning hatred of Japan and things Japanese such as has not survived anywhere else in Asia, or for that matter, in Europe. Japan, with the exception of these few, post-war years, has always been independent: the Philippines used to be an American colony (although the Americans, thanks to their traditional anti-colonialist sentiments, do not like to call their colonies 'colonies'). Japan is an over-populated Empire: the Philippines are an under-populated Republican archipelago of more than 7,000 islands and seventy languages.

It is not easy for the visitor to grasp the significance of these last mentioned geographical and linguistic facts. Seven

thousand islands and seventy languages . . . Europeans, as a
rule, do not make any special effort to find out much about
this particular spot of South-East Asia. It is true that some
of the major islands such as Luzon (with Manila, the capital),
and Mindanao, as well as the names of Bataan and Corre-
gidor, became world-famous during the last war. Yet, the
Philippines are off the beaten track: for Europeans they look
like rather third-rate Europe; for the Americans they are a
lost colony – so the Filipinos are neglected, if not forgotten.
They feel rather strongly about this and this is the first
reason for their being an Angry Young Nation.

The Philippines extend over a length of 1,158 miles, and
a breadth of 688 miles, yet the area of the whole territory
is a little smaller than that of Britain. It cannot possibly be a
bureaucrat's paradise to administrate a country of 7,083
islands of which only 466 have an area of one square mile or
more and only 2,400 or so have names. All the same, the
Philippine Islands still remain a model of unity and bureau-
cratic efficiency compared with their neighbour, Indonesia.

The first painful impression of the visitor to this otherwise
very agreeable country is that it is one of the most expensive
places in the world. In fact, it takes second place only to
the record-holder, Venezuela. A mediocre meal costs £2
and a whisky 10s, just to mention two essentials. Having
decided to cut your stay a little shorter than you intended,
you go out for a walk in the beautiful city of Manila. It is
all very pleasant but the feeling slowly grows on you that
Manila might easily be transferred without much adjust-
ment to, say, Colorado. When you get to know the place a
little better, you find traces of manifold influences: Spanish,
Japanese, even English and, first of all, as I have already
mentioned, American.

The English influence is very slight. Yet, an invasion by Sir
Francis Drake in 1577 is remembered almost nostalgically.
The influence of Spain, on the other hand, is ubiquitous.

The very name of the Islands was given in honour of His Most Catholic Majesty, Philip II. Many villages and streets bear Spanish names; Manila's Regent Street-cum-Bond Street-cum-Fifth Avenue, for example, is called Escolta. People have Spanish names, too, and many of them have Spanish faces. They are – with few exceptions – all Catholics and devout Catholics at that. They have rather Spanish manners and are still unable to appear anywhere on time. 'Punctuality is the courtesy of the vulgar,' they hold. And these friendly and hospitable people are still as fiesta-minded as the Spaniards. They hold fiestas on the slightest provocation and as the Catholic Church is not noticeably poor in patron saints for absolutely everything under the sun, provocation is not lacking. For the fiestas people must have food and some money and – just like the Spaniards – the Filipino will not think twice before pawning his bedding or going hungry for a week in order to do justice to the occasion. But few people speak Spanish nowadays; and Spanish influence is mostly concentrated in Luzon. The memory of Spain, connected as it is with ruthlessness and oppression, is not too popular.

Japan is hated. The occupation with its cruelty, pillage, rape and other horrors is not easily forgotten. In Siam or Malaya the Japanese occupation was just a passing phase; in the Philippines it was a psychological and historical event of the first magnitude. Psychological because it engendered hatred and bitterness: a hatred and bitterness which must have been long stored up in the soul of the people and which now found an outlet against the cruel invader. But the occupation was also a great historical event, because ultimately it led to independence. The Japanese – harsh masters as they were – were nevertheless Asians. They defeated and humiliated the American master-race and inspired and disillusioned the Filipinos at one and the same time. The Filipinos realised for the first time that the Americans could, after all, be beaten by Asians; but they also experienced the kind of freedom which this liberation by Asians brought in its train. 'We are Asians,' the Filipinos have now, after some hesitation, decided, 'and we accept our common destiny with Japan. But we definitely do not accept Japan's leadership.' (People all over the world are given to uttering phrases like 'common destiny'. There is no earthly reason, in fact, why the Philippines should share Japan's destiny or vice versa.)

Probably the most lasting and certainly the most conspicuous influence of all is the American. You find plenty of bowling alleys in Manila with large notices at the entrance:

DEPOSIT YOUR FIRE-ARMS WITH THE MANAGER

The Constitution is drawn up on the American pattern. There is little to distinguish between the programmes of the various political parties, it all reduces mainly to a fight between personalities. There is no effective Socialist Party. A Socialist is regarded as a Communist and the Communist Party is banned. The Americans founded many welfare and cultural institutions and, most important of all, an excellent educational system. Literacy gained enormous ground during the period of American rule. Filipinos claim that 85 per cent of the population is now literate. This claim seems to be a little far-fetched, but there is no doubt that a great many things have improved since the Americans took over at the turn of this century.

The main trouble with the Americans – at least in the eyes of the young nationalist and intellectuals – is that in spite of the fact they are supposed to have gone, they are still there.

'Our independence is a sham,' I was told by a young

writer. 'Perhaps the Americans cannot help it. Perhaps this is the fate of every small nation. They have gone but they are still here and not only at their military bases. We are a sovereign state but our economy is entirely dependent on them. That's what has turned us really into an Angry Young Nation.'

The Americans, always generous with both hands, are masters, at the same time, of the art of treading on other people's corns. A U.S. sailor, George Roe, was accused by the Philippine authorities of the crime of 'homicide by neglect'. The alleged victim was a young Filipino girl. Roe, however, before his trial, was smuggled out of the country by the U.S. Navy. This stupid and furtive act created more ill-feeling than other, more important, moves. A small group of people went to picket the American Embassy with notices: WE DON'T WANT A ROE DEAL. The matter and the demonstration were, however, hushed up by the Philippine authorities. While the execution of Jose Rizal by the Spaniards served in the end only to create national enthusiasm, unity and an immortal legend, the Roe incident and similar affairs create only a feeling that the Philippines are not handled even with the pretence of equality by the United States and that the Philippines themselves are taking part in a vast game of make-believe by trying to play the part of an independent nation.

The young intellectuals also resent American propaganda.

'They're trying to sell us the "American way of life", with the same aggressive salesmanship as they sell refrigerators or life-insurance policies. I wish, in a way, they could succeed in this. But at least another hundred years must pass before the Philippines can afford the American way of life.'

These views, I repeat, are the views of a grumbling but thoughtful minority. The majority is quite happy to imitate the most easily exportable insignia of the 'American way of life', their manners, their coloured neckties, their crew-cuts, etc. They embrace a juke-box and ice-cream-soda civilisation with relish. Quite a few of them grow rich and then they can afford to be much more American than the Americans themselves.

'There is a growing social layer here,' another Filipino I met remarked contemptuously, 'which fell from the coconut tree straight into a Cadillac.'

American influence is exerted, however, most strongly on thought and language. The twenty million inhabitants of the islands have about seventy native tongues which is, in a sense, considerably less than having one. Even the main languages of the islands, indeed, their very names are completely unknown to most Europeans: I certainly had never heard of them before my visit. Sugbuanon, Iloko, Bikol and Samarnon are not among the major forces of civilisation, nor is even Tagalog, the most widespread and most cultivated of the native tongues, which was successfully raised by the anti-Spanish revolutionary organisation, Katipunan, to the dignity of national language. Tagalog boasts of a famous epic poem, *Florante at Laura*, by Francisco Balagitas, which is a veiled attack on Spanish rule. There are also some newspapers and magazines appearing in the language, but practically no books are published in Tagalog at all. English is the real – although not the official – national language of the Philippines. Many nationalists are trying to unlearn English. They work hard at it but with limited success only. English is a language much easier to learn than to forget. And a large number of young people – ardent nationalists though they may be – refuse to cut themselves off from the trend of civilisation and retreat into the mysteries of Tagalog or Iloko.

Nevertheless, the language problem is a sore one. I spent my last evening in Manila in the company of the Angry

Young Men of this Angry Young Nation. One of them said, and all the others heartily agreed:

'To write in English is a tremendous advantage – but only on paper. Why? I don't know. Perhaps it *is* difficult, after all, to take a Filipino writer seriously. One can listen to a Japanese or an Indian writer but, apparently, not to a Filipino. Maybe it is because we are so accessible; because we write in English. We are not exotic enough. Do you know that the Philippines are the third largest English-speaking country in the world? And do you know that not one single Philippine book has ever appeared in England or in the United States?'

(These statements sounded a little fantastic. The Philippines are indeed the 'third largest English-speaking country in the world', if you take the whole British Commonwealth of Nations, including all the Dominions and colonies, as one single country. It is not true that no Philippine work has ever been published in the United States – few and far between though these publications have been; I believe, however, that nothing by a Philippine writer has ever been published in England.)

My young companions united Spanish charm and the quiet pleasantness of the Malay with an intellectual curiosity entirely their own. They knew more of the latest literary trends and fashions in England than I. They were keen, brilliantly intelligent and not bitter, but resigned to living on a suburban archipelago.

'We've taken over the protection racket system from the United States,' said my friend whom I have already quoted. 'People are sometimes murdered here for no obvious reason and the killers are never caught. Landowners often employ armed guards to protect them against their own peasants. Salaries are low. Some of our politicians were found to have invested public money for private gain but no one was very agitated about this and they got away with it when they explained that "they meant to pay it back". Criminal cases are often "settled" between magistrates and the parties in private before they come for trial. But there is nothing wrong with our people – the authorities tell us – because we all go to Mass at six o'clock every morning. And many of us two or three times afterwards.'

Before our party broke up in the early hours of the morning, one of my young friends summed up their problems:

'We write in English and try to be English writers. We are Malays who cannot quite make up their minds whether to remain Spanish or become Americans. And we are an independent nation whose main problem is how to achieve independence.'

HONG KONG

NO ESCAPE FROM DESTINY

By the end of my first day there, I had fallen in love with Hong Kong. As has befallen many other middle-aged men before me, I loved her for her beauty, which is breathtaking, out of this world. Hong Kong with its harbour, its green mountains and white houses, its blue sky and still bluer sea, its Chinese streets, is the loveliest place I have ever seen in my life. It is a particularly happy blend of the Riviera and the Bay of Naples, only – to my taste – better than either and the exotic flavour adds beauty. Istanbul with the Bosphorus is the runner-up on my own list, though definitely in second place. (I have never seen Rio de Janeiro which, I understand, is Hong Kong's only serious rival.)

And again, like many other middle-aged lovers before me, I was perfectly right to fall in love with sheer beauty. 'A wife is sought for her virtue, a concubine for her beauty,' says the Chinese proverb. I did not want to marry Hong

Kong (though what's wrong with a beautiful wife?). I
wanted her as a concubine.

By the end of my first day, it was becoming clear to me
that the object of my love suffered from some ugly disfigure-
ments. But I loved her all the same – even with her warts.
In fact, I loved some of the warts themselves.

Emerging from the airport building, I looked round for
a taxi. None was visible but I spotted a huge, American,
chauffeur-driven, private limousine. A young, well-dressed
Chinese approached me and asked me where I was going
to stay.

'At the Gloucester,' I replied.

'In that case, you need not look for a taxi,' he said. 'This
car is waiting for you.'

I asked him if he was an airport official. He shook his
head and smiled mysteriously. Did the car belong to the
Gloucester Hotel? He smiled again.

'No. This is my car. It is waiting for you.'

'Without experience one gains no wisdom.' I murmured
the ancient Chinese proverb to myself and got in. As soon
as we started off, the young man asked me whether this was
my first visit to Hong Kong? And to the Orient? I answered
both queries in the affirmative and my friend, having gathered
the valuable piece of intelligence that I was what our American brethren call a sucker, seemed satisfied. Learning that I
wanted to change some money, as I did not have one single
Hong Kong dollar, he instructed the chauffeur to stop in
front of a money-changer's, got out with me and saw to it
that I was given the most advantageous rate of exchange.
We got back into the car; I still had no idea who on earth
my anonymous benefactor might be. He asked me whether I
wanted any suits made, like everyone else who came to
Hong Kong. Because he was a tailor. I knew that Hong
Kong was famous for the cheapness of the best English
materials, the skill of the Shanghai tailors who rival those

of Savile Row, and also for their speed which definitely
leaves Savile Row nowhere. They come to measure you at
eight o'clock in the morning, take a first fitting at eleven, a
second fitting at three, and a faultless suit is delivered at
five-thirty. I knew that everyone, absolutely everyone, who
came to Hong Kong has a few suits made; but I decided
that I was going to be the exception. I am not a dandy. In
fact, I do not care in the least what I am wearing as long as
my garments cover my body and keep me warm. I was not
inclined to spend my time arguing with tailors and waiting
for fittings. So I paid rather scant attention to my Chinese
friend who told me that he had provided me with his car
and his friendly assistance in the hope that he might have
the privilege of making a few suits for me; because, he added
– cautiously but with some conviction in his voice – he could
easily make better suits than the one I was actually wearing.
I answered with an old Chinese proverb: 'You may change
the clothes; you cannot change the man,' and added that I
would see.

All this happened in Kowloon, at the tip of the Chinese
mainland. From there I had to cross over to Hong Kong
island. My tailor-friend, a former refugee from Shanghai
who had arrived here about five years before, put me on the
ferry, gave me his card, and bade me farewell. A Chinese
gentleman sitting next to me in the ferry asked whether I
was in search of a tailor because, as it happened, he knew a
very good one. Arriving in Hong Kong – in Victoria, the
capital, to be precise – I was offered further tailors by the
coolie who carried my luggage to the hotel; the liftman;
and by the boy who led me to my room. I expected to find
printed instructions in my room: 'Ring once for the maid;
twice for the waiter; three times for a tailor.' Ringing, I soon
found, was quite unnecessary. The waiter appeared unsum-
moned and enquired whether I needed a tailor. I replied
with a polite but firm *no*. He bowed and left. Five minutes

later there was a knock on my door. It was a tailor anxious
to know whether I needed his services. I whispered the
Chinese proverb to myself: 'Man can cure disease but not
fate', and said, indeed yes, I wanted a tailor badly and
ordered three suits from him there and then.

PARADISE WITH WARTS

I went out for a walk and I found myself loving Hong Kong
more every minute. Hong Kong is the last survivor of the
fabulous Chinese cities of a bygone age. The very idea of
being in a Chinese town stirred me: I admired the beautiful
and enigmatic Chinese characters and I loved their exotic
faces. I knew, of course, that my face was just as exotic to
the Chinese as theirs was to me; and I also knew that it was
no great pleasure for them to see *my* exotic face. But my
heart overflowed towards them, one and all.

Hong Kong is truly a shoppers' paradise, probably
unrivalled anywhere in the world. It is also a free port;
there is no duty on anything. Leicas are cheaper than in Ger-
many; Cannons (Japanese Leicas) cheaper than in Japan;
watches than in Switzerland; perfume and brandy than in
France; textiles than in Lancashire. While I was there, a
U.S. destroyer came in. The crew spent 750,000 U.S. dollars
in three days. I spent less. But before you could say Jack
Robinson of Ching Fu Tang, I had bought a pair of
enormous binoculars for £5. Considering that I have never
been at a horse race in my life and have no intention of
going in the next forty years if I can help it, nor do I keep
a yacht just now, I was a little puzzled why I needed those
binoculars. But I was not the first person to be ruined by
Hong Kong's irresistible bargain prices. I did not blame
myself. 'A wise man will not reprove a fool,' I said with the
old Chinese proverb while studying the distant and beautiful

shores of Kowloon with my newly acquired binoculars. Then
I thought of another Chinese proverb: 'Even he who has
accumulated ten thousand taels of silver cannot take with
him at death half a copper cash.' So I heaved a deep sigh
and entered a shop to buy presents for my family.

Money flows freely in Hong Kong. The Chinese women –
with their tight silk dresses slit high on both sides and
showing their thighs, but always covering their necks – are
very attractive: the dance halls are full; food is as good as
in Paris but more varied; the weather is fair; life is easy and
servants are cheap. But for whom is life easy? I asked myself.
And what if you do not *need* cheap servants; what if you *are*
a cheap servant yourself?

There is, of course, a very different side to all this
pleasantness. You cannot help noticing Hong Kong's warts
almost as soon as you see its miraculous beauty. You see too
many poor, wretchedly poor, people in the streets. How slim
the Chinese are, I thought, until I realised that these people
were not simply thin or slim but emaciated with opium. I
kept remembering the man who had carried my luggage
from the ferry to the hotel. I had felt acute embarrassment
all the time and avoided the eyes of people passing by. And
then, suddenly, I stopped and gaped at the first rickshaw
I had ever seen. A fat Chinese was leaning back in the
rickshaw, reading a newspaper, while a thin Chinese, running as fast as he could, in fact galloping like a horse, pulled
the rickshaw. In the rain, as I was to see later, the passenger
is protected while the rickshaw coolie, running in his bare
feet, splashes through the pools of water. Another day I
saw a coolie running uphill with a heavy load under the
scorching sun.

One day a Chinese friend of mine suggested that we take
a rickshaw. I refused and he saw by my face that I was
rather horrified at the idea.

'I know you sensitive European intellectuals with a so-

D

called conscience and a so-called guilt complex,' he said. 'Bertrand Russell himself refused one day to travel by rickshaw until it was explained to him that, if we all refused, the poor rickshaw coolies would starve.'

'You had to explain that to Bertrand Russell?' I asked. My friend gave no reply.

'Little boys of six,' I reminded him, 'in early Victorian England, earned their living by going down chimneys to sweep them. And by working in factories for twelve hours a day. They were no carefree amateurs, either. They lived on it; and they also died on it.'

'So what do you suggest?' he asked. 'What's the solution? Should the rickshaws be abolished?'

'Of course,' I said. 'They should. Such a thing debases a whole community.'

'But you can't abolish the rickshaws,' he replied. 'There would be a revolt.'

'Who would revolt?'

'The rickshaw coolies, of course. Being a rickshaw coolie is a good, secure and envied job.'

I saw people – often old women – carrying enormous loads on a long stick on their shoulder; I saw people sitting on the pavement having their meals. There was a child of about five feeding another child of two, obviously his brother. The elder held his two chopsticks in one hand and a bowl of rice in the other. From this he had a mouthful himself, then gave a mouthful to his brother. He was scrupulously honest: he never took more than he had given the little fellow although he often had to wait until the latter had swallowed his mouthful. Soon he came to the last chopstickful. He looked at the little boy, at the empty bowl, and at the last morsel of rice. He hesitated. Then he gave it to his brother. He was himself, as I have said, about five years old.

It was long past midnight before I thought of returning to my hotel. I was walking along a narrow, rather dark street nearby, when I suddenly tripped over something. It was an old man with long, white side-whiskers, sleeping on the stones.

'*Parlez-vous français?*' he asked me without opening his eyes.

I stopped and said nothing.

'Can I direct you to a good tailor, sir?' he asked again, sitting up, still half asleep.

I am sure it was very funny. But I did not laugh.

THE SQUATTERS

But Hong Kong is, for all that, a Paradise. That is why so many poor people live there. Life in Hong Kong is better than it is in China, so refugees keep pouring in.

The little, rocky island of Hong Kong was occupied by the British in 1841 as an episode of the Opium War. Its population then consisted of a few hundred poor farmers, fishermen, and stone-cutters with a fair sprinkling of pirates among them. The Treaty of Nanking in 1842 formally recognised the 'perpetual cession' of the Island. Its capital, Victoria, was soon established and became prosperous. In 1860 three and a half square miles of territory on the mainland of Kowloon along with Stonecutters Island were ceded to Great Britain, also 'in perpetuity'. Finally in 1898 a further district – the largest of all – and some additional islands, together named the New Territories, were leased from China for ninety-nine years. The total present-day territory of the colony of Hong Kong is 391 square miles, about one-twentieth the size of Wales. These piecemeal acquisitions resulted in some confusion in nomenclature as well as in a paradox. The confusion is that when people speak of Hong Kong, they sometimes mean the city of Victoria, sometimes the island of Hong Kong, sometimes the entire colony. (All more or less correct, of course, as long as it is clear exactly what you have in mind.) As to the paradox: the lease of the New Territories expires in 1997, not quite four decades from now. No one knows whether China will renew the lease or not, not even China herself. But everybody knows without a shadow of doubt that the rest of the colony cannot survive without the New Territories whence Hong Kong and Kowloon draw their water supply. Yet, no one seems to be giving a thought to the possibility that Hong Kong may be lost in thirty-nine years, to say nothing of even sooner. The building of blocks of flats, houses for refugees and new factories is going ahead with speed and energy. Rich people escape from Shanghai and Peking and, instead of getting as far away from China as possible as one would expect, they settle in Hong Kong and invest all their money there. Why is this? A high ranking official of the Hong Kong government told me thoughtfully: 'We don't know what's going to happen. We have no policy. But it will turn out in one way or another.' I was proud of him; that's the spirit.

The malarial and pirate-infested island soon became the most beautiful, prosperous and famous port and mercantile centre in East Asia with a population numbering nearly a million before World War II. Hong Kong was attacked by the Japanese almost simultaneously with Pearl Harbour, and occupied. By the time the Japanese evacuated it, about half the population had gone and the place was dilapidated and melancholy. Hundreds of thousands of Chinese had simply walked out and the Japanese were glad to see them go; it meant that they did not have to feed them. I do not think there is one other spot on the globe where population has been subject to such wild fluctuations as that of Hong Kong: just under a million before the war; about half a million after the war and two and a half million today. The equivalent figures in Greater London would be about twelve million before the war, six million after it, and thirty million today.

It was round about 1947 that the first anti-Communist refugees arrived: prosperous businessmen, mostly from Shanghai, who had anticipated the Communist conquest of China. They brought their money, their business, and their skilled labourers with them. As time went on, more and more came – poorer and poorer people. Immigration became a flood in 1949. In the end, the wretched, the poor, and the starving far outnumbered the well-to-do. By 1950 the situation had become desperate and Hong Kong closed its doors.

The doors remained closed for a long time. Only a small number of people were let in on a quota basis. Peking, too, forcibly prevented people from coming over. Trying to escape to Hong Kong was regarded as treason. Then, from 1951 onwards, quite large numbers of people started returning to China from the colony. It seemed as if China was winning the Korean war; and all Chinese, however anti-Communist, started feeling proud of her; China's prestige was very much in the ascendant; the theory that 'the Communists were not so bad, after all,' began to gain ground.

In 1956 China suddenly changed her policy and made an offer to the government of Hong Kong! Chinese domiciled in Hong Kong who wanted to visit their relations in China would be allowed to do so even without proper passports, provided the Hong Kong government, on its part, would accept visiting Chinese. It sounded very reasonable; so Hong Kong accepted, whereupon, in the next eight months, a quarter of a million Hong Kong Chinese went to China and all returned while 80,000 Chinese Chinese came to Hong Kong and 70,000 of them stayed there for good. No one has been able to stem the flood since then. Immigrants are no longer admitted officially, but illegal immigration is ceaseless – about 15,000 people arrive every month.

About a hundred would-be immigrants are picked up every night by the Hong Kong police and returned. The Communist authorities shrug their shoulders, the would-be refugees are not punished, indeed, they are promptly turned loose to try again. Once they are across the frontier they merge into the mass and no one can ever trace them. Even when detected, they are no longer sent back. There is also a great influx from Macao, the neighbouring Portuguese colony. People from Macao have free entry into Hong Kong, consequently the manufacture of faked Portuguese papers has become one of the major industries. The reason for the immigration, by the way, is mostly economic, not political. It is not so much freedom of speech or freedom of worship these people seek; it is simply more food.

More food they often do not find – or not very quickly, at any rate. Hong Kong is no more able to accommodate this vast increase in its post-war population than London or New York would be. So squatters soon sprouted like mushrooms all over the place. 'Their need was so great and pressing,' says a little official pamphlet, *A Problem of People*, 'that they had no thought for the ownership of land and it would have required an army of police to restrain them. Virtually every sizeable vacant site which was not under some form of physical or continuing protection was occupied and when there was no flat land remaining they moved up to the hillsides and colonised the ravines and slopes which were too steep for natural development. The huts were constructed of such material as they could lay hands on at little or no cost – flattened sheets of tin, wooden boarding, cardboard, sacking slung on frames – every variety of two-dimensional material that was light enough to carry and cheap enough to beg or steal or buy for a few dollars.'

Land was scarce and the squatters were horribly over-crowded. On an average, there were six people to a tiny hut. There was no sanitation and no system of refuse collection.

The stench of these filthy and disease-ridden communities
was pestilential. Such water as there was had to be carried
from long distances. I myself saw women washing their linen
in the gutter. Chickens, ducks, and pigs often shared the
huts with the human population. Some of the squatters
worked in the town, others started cottage industries and
often managed to equip their hovels as small factories.
Smuggling and manufacturing drugs, keeping brothels and
gambling houses and providing hideouts for fugitive criminals
were all normal occupations among Hong Kong's half a
million squatters. But there were, of course, shining examples
of courage, resolution and resourcefulness, too, in fact, all
the vices and all the virtues flourished in the huts – just as
in other human communities. From time to time huge fires
swept away thousands of these huts built of cardboard and
sacks and the inhabitants, as the saying goes, lost all their
possessions. But the Chinese, in contrast with most other
people, do not complain, whine and blame others in such
a situation. While the fires were still raging they were already
busy building new, and even more wretched huts, this time
on top of flat-roofed houses or in the streets, in front of other
buildings.

The authorities have been building huge tenement dwell-
ings for the refugees for some time and hundreds of thousands
of the former squatters are now 'properly' housed. That
means five in a room, but at least there is proper sanitation
in the new houses and they are reasonably fireproof. The
British Government – according to the retiring Governor –
praised the Hong Kong government's heroic and almost
superhuman efforts in generous terms; but sent no money
to help it. Hundreds of thousands of refugees are still
squatting on the hillsides and rooftops; and, as I have mentioned, about 15,000 new immigrants arrive every month.
Some newcomers have relations in Hong Kong and they
are always given shelter – no matter how many they are

and no matter what hardship they cause their hosts. A friend of mine, a French journalist, once discovered that eleven Chinese were sharing his cook's small room. He liked his cook and knew the unbreakable law of hospitality to relations, so he acted as though he had noticed nothing. After all, you can easily overlook eleven resident guests in a three-roomed flat. Many a newcomer, however, who has no relations at all, builds a new hut on the hillside and his fondest dream is that one day, perhaps, he may share it with his own pig.

They all live somehow and they all find some sort of work or means of livelihood. The normal working day in Hong Kong is nine hours on all seven days in the week. (In European-owned factories it is slightly easier.) There is no agitation for a six-day working week.

A friend of mine, a Hungarian poet, who spent three years in a Communist concentration camp in Hungary, once told me that it was not the loss of freedom which was the most intolerable part of his experience; not the beatings; not the terrible food; not the cold; not even the work in the stone quarry; but the fact that they had been forced to work seven days a week, month after month, year after year. With a day's rest here and there – he said – it might have been bearable but as it was their life expectation was estimated at two years. Yet, in Hong Kong, it is the workers themselves who protest against any protective legislation. A six-day working week would mean the loss of a day's earnings; if women were not allowed to go on night-shift their families might suffer irreparable loss. So they insist on their right to work themselves to death. And still they come, still they pour in from across those mysterious borders.

LU-WU

One day I drove to Lu Wu Bridge on the Chinese frontier.

The world – so the saying goes – is getting smaller every day. Maybe. But it is also getting larger. A few years ago you could still get a train in Kowloon, travel for seventeen days and arrive at Victoria (not Victoria, Hong Kong, but Victoria Station, London). Today you can travel twenty-one miles from Kowloon, arrive at the frontier and get out. No passenger train crosses the frontier.

But you can change at the border and go on to Canton. I saw the international coolies, wearing red straw hats, carrying luggage belonging to some French diplomats. I also saw the Red flag and the Red star on the Chinese side. I saw the stone-faced Red soldiers and our Hong Kong Chinese, standing opposite each other without exchanging one single word in days, weeks, months, years. Even the Jews and Arabs have human relationship at the Mandelbaum Gate in Jerusalem. I watched the local Chinese population crossing, carrying their bundles on shoulder yokes. And I had a long, long look with my newly acquired binoculars into the depths of Red China.

On my return to Hong Kong, I informed one of the government officials that I was going to write a book on the problems of China.

'Go ahead,' he said. 'You have at least seen it with your binoculars. Many people have written books on China with much less experience.'

Then he asked: 'And what will you call the book?'

'Oh,' I replied, 'it will be the first of a series. I'll call it *Outside China*.'

MY COLONY

Hong Kong, I repeat, is a wonderful place in spite of all its poverty. I shall never retire if I can help it: I want to die either with pen or with binoculars in hand. But if I change my mind, it is here in Hong Kong that I shall retire. Not

as a squatter – somehow one never pictures oneself as a
squatter – but as a well-to-do, middle-class, one-thing-or-
another. I should have a little house high up on the hill – I
understand, the higher up you are, the better it is for your
self-esteem – with the loveliest view on earth to look at. I
should often take a sampan at Aberdeen, the nearby fishing
village, and go out to one of the two floating restaurants to
eat female crab with Chinese vinegar, garoupe (their delicious white fish) with chili, pepper and onions, ginger and
sweet-sour sauce, and finish up with swallow-nest soup.
Coming home after midnight, I should throw a glance at
the squatters' settlements, and near the Kowloon ferry I
should pause to watch the hundreds of people in search of
a night's rest and in search of a dream looking for a cosy
corner on the pavement, or an empty and unguarded boat.
And then, perhaps, as time went on, I should slowly forget
all those people who cannot afford female crab with Chinese
vinegar and I'd have a wonderful time.

It was not until my last day there that I started to ponder
the question: why did I love Hong Kong so very much? It
is indeed beautiful; it is elegant; it is prosperous in spite of
all its misery; it is hard-working, happy in its own way; it
is charming and evocative. But none of this was the answer
to my question.

Then suddenly I understood. For all the exotic glamour
of the place, it was home. It was 9,000 miles away from
England, yet it was a bit of England. There were Chinese
characters all around me, Chinese faces, Chinese food in the
restaurants and Chinese rickshaw coolies in the street, junks
in the harbour – some graceful, some hideous – but British
bobbies on the street corners and English cleanliness in the
main streets. Somewhere, deep down, you cannot help feeling that China is distant, mysterious, and dangerous. But
how can Hong Kong be mysterious and dangerous when
it has English-type traffic-lights, just like Hove or Scar-

borough? I was at home, in my own colony. And I also knew that I had found myself out, at last. Somewhere, at the bottom of my heart, I must have resented the fact that Britain was busy losing her Empire just when she gained me. We all have a secret imperialist-complex, undiscovered even by Freud. Here, at last, I was in a place where I could be a colonialist with a clear conscience. Here, no one wants the British to leave. The Hong Kong Chinese want them to stay; the Chinese Chinese want them to stay (because Hong Kong is their main window on the West, as well as a profitable source of hard currency); even the Americans with the laudable anti-colonialist fervour of an ex-colony, want them to stay. Hong Kong is a colony whole-heartedly in favour of colonisation.

Before I could engender too much warmth for these newly-found sentiments of mine, I met a young Englishman – a charming and civilised chap – who said to me:

'I am really broad-minded and very cosmopolitan. I mix here with all the races I can find: English, French, Americans, Germans, Japanese . . .'

I looked at him in amazement. I said to him: 'Say that just once again.'

He repeated word by word what he had said.

It had completely slipped his memory that there are Chinese, too, in Hong Kong.

* * *

Before leaving my colony I threw another uneasy glance in the direction of the frontier. I remembered the ancient Chinese proverb: 'When your fortune is good, you rule over the devils; when your fortune is bad, they rule over you.' Then I also remembered some statistics about the annual increase of the Chinese population and made some quick calculations. The net increase in the population of China *per minute* is a hundred souls. There are about 1,500 more little Chinese in this world, oh Reader, than there were when you began to read this chapter.

But I was not really perturbed. I thought of an ancient English proverb: 'We'll muddle through somehow.'

MALAYA

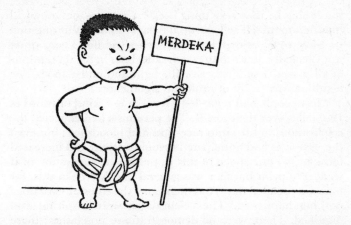

THE IMPORTANCE OF BEING IN PRISON

I arrived in Kuala Lumpur very soon after the day of
Merdeka, i.e. the achievement of independence. Malaya
was then the youngest independent state in the world and
I am sure I ought to have been moved by deep and elevating
thoughts. But during the first days of my stay I kept thinking
of an old yellow newspaper cutting I have had in my
possession for over twenty years. I had cut it out of a Budapest evening paper in the mid-'thirties and cherished it ever
since because I thought it the worst headline in the history
of journalism. It was printed in the largest and blackest type:
NO SENSATIONAL EVENT HAS OCCURRED
TODAY. The four evening papers of Budapest were
engaged in cut-throat competition in those days and each
felt duty-bound to provide its readers with a breath-taking
and exclusive headline every day. Some major political
bombshell (I forget what exactly) must have been expected
for the day in question but the bomb, apparently, had failed
to explode. Hence the headline. 'How can the absence of

something be that very thing itself?' I put the metaphysical question to myself as I cut up the page. I posed this question in May 1936, and it has remained a riddle. Then, quite unexpectedly, more than two decades later in Kuala Lumpur of all places, I suddenly saw the light and understood. The headline was really of profound significance.

Most people had regarded Merdeka as a kind of sword of Damocles over their heads. The pessimists had expected the celebrations to turn into race-riots and bloodshed; but even the optimists had anticipated demonstrations and increased tension. No one spoke of this in public, no suggestion of it went into print but fear was general and Merdeka was, for many, a dreaded day. And then came the colossal sensation: nothing happened. The celebrations were inspiring and dignified. There were no demonstrations, no clashes: there was general rejoicing: NO SENSATIONAL EVENT HAS OCCURRED TODAY.

* * *

Why not? Well, things are seldom what they seem. The achievement of independence was not really the achievement of independence for two diametrically opposed reasons. First, no state can be really independent nowadays. It can be as independent as, say, Great Britain but no more. Secondly, even within the limits of possibility, Malaya did not become independent on August 31, 1957: to all intents and purposes it had been independent for the two or three preceding years. Merdeka was the formal celebration of Malaya's becoming something it did not really become; and also for becoming something it had already been.

Then, again, the achievement of independence was an anti-climax for many. It all went too smoothly, too rapidly – and this was the fault of the British. The idea of Malayan independence gathered momentum in the post-war years. During the war the Japanese invaders were hated for their

brutality, yet, at the same time, they stirred Malaya to a
new Asian consciousness. Japan may have been brutal but
she destroyed the belief in the invincibility of the White
Man. So Malaya asked for her independence. And Britain
nodded and granted her independence. It was too disappointing. What can you do with people like the British?

The unfortunate Malay leaders were thus deprived of
their chance of spending long spells in prison and otherwise
suffering for their country. They would no doubt have
endured imprisonment as bravely as the Indians but they
were less lucky. This unfortunate fact diminishes their popu-
larity in many youthful eyes. Now the Queen of England
has been replaced by a Malay king; the British ruling class by
a Malay ruling class; the excellent and efficient administration – trained and built up by the British – goes on doing its
excellent and efficient work exactly as before. Some people
keep hinting at the desirability of real changes but they are
not too numerous. The 'Emergency' – declared during the
Communist bid for power and connected with many horrible
and tragic incidents – is slowly receding into the background. The country is prosperous, indeed rich. So where
is Malaya to find her problems? How can she solve burning
questions if she cannot find any? Where can she find real
difficulties to worry about?

All this is not easy. The rest of the world has much more
experience in such matters than the new state of Malaya.
Europeans, Americans and Russians are wonderful at
creating problems and tensions from almost nothing; they
can always conjure up a world crisis from the magic top-hat
of international relations. The Malayans watch with some
slight envy. 'No problems,' they sigh. 'Or at least not enough
of them. That's our trouble. What are we to do? Well, we
must get along without them as best we can. A pity, but
there it is!'

Luckily, there are *some* problems.

Malaya is supposed to be a country of Malays but it isn't really. (Before going any further, I had better define certain terms. A *Malayan* is an inhabitant of Malaya, irrespective of race or creed; a *Malay* is a member of the Malay race and a Moslem; while a *Malaysian* comes from the common stock of Malays and Indonesians. So, for example, a Chinese can be a Malayan but he cannot be a Malay any more than a Malay can be a Chinese. A Malay can also be a Malayan and so can an Indian but the Indian can never be a Malaysian. And so on. I shall open classes for more advanced pupils in the autumn.) The Malays are pleasant, kind, smiling people. They are full of goodwill, they are amicable and hospitable. It is mostly their endearing temperament but partly also their laziness which prevents them from violent action and fierce political passions. The main problem of Malaya is a shortage of Malays. There are too many Chinese in China; there are too many Indians in India; but there are not enough Malays in Malaya. Official statistics assure you that there are *nearly* three million Malaysians but *more* than three million others – Chinese, Indians and Europeans. But Malaysians, as I have clearly explained, are not all Malays. All one can fairly say is that the Malays form the largest single group in their country. Even this, however, remains only true as long as Singapore remains a separate unit, a British colony. If you add Singapore's one and a quarter million to Malay's population with its more than 900,000 Chinese then the Malays no longer find themselves even as the largest single group.

The 'shortage of Malays' is both absolute and relative; and it also means an almost complete absence of a Malay middle class. The Sultans, the aristocracy, the top layer of society and the civil service are Malays; so are many of the

road-sweepers, navvies and taxi-drivers. And, first of all,
the peasants, populating the many *kampongs*, wearing the
inevitable *sarong* and the equally inevitable friendly smile
on their lips. But the number of independent Malay lawyers,
doctors and accountants (the three put together, I mean)
in Kuala Lumpur is under half a dozen. There are not
enough Malay undergraduates at the university. You will
not find a Malay hotel among the 156 hotels of Kuala
Lumpur and not one really good Malay restaurant in the
capital of Malaya. The absence of a good Malay restaurant,
it should be added, is also due to the fact that the Malays
dislike eating in public as much as the Chinese love it. The
Malay kitchen has a wonderful speciality, the *satay* (small
chunks of beef on coconut stalks, roasted in a spicy sauce
over charcoal). You go and eat *satay* in Chinese restaurants.

Certain new laws relating to immigration, land tenure
and appointments to the civil service are designed to secure
the supremacy of the Malays in their own country.

I liked Malaya very much but I suffered two bitter
disappointments on the very first day. I had known two
Malay words before my arrival: *kampong* and *tiffin*. (*Tiffin*, I
found out later, was not really Malayan.) So I wanted to
see a *kampong* (a Malay village) and have *tiffin*.

The first morning after my arrival a friend drove me from
Singapore to a *kampong* on the mainland, in Johore. We
went through Johore Bahru, the capital of that state, and
reached the village.

'Is this a typical Malay *kampong*?' I asked.

My friend shook his head. 'No. Not a very typical one.'

'What's wrong with it?' I enquired.

'There is nothing really wrong with it,' he explained. 'But
you see, *all* the people in this village are employed by the
B.B.C.' After some reflection he added: 'Which is not truly
typical of the whole of Malaya.'

He looked guilty.

He took me home for *tiffin*. And then I suffered my second disappointment. *Tiffin* is an excellent meal. But it is dangerously like lunch.

*   *   *

The Chinese in Malaya occupy a unique position. I know of no other country where the entire middle class has been imported from abroad. Nor has the Malayan brand of perfect division of labour any parallel anywhere else: the Malay upper classes hold almost all the political power; but economic power is entirely in the hands of the Chinese.

The Chinese have a deep-rooted complex, as have many other people (probably including myself) who belong neither here nor there. These Chinese live in Malaya but they are not Malays; on the other hand, as they have lived in Malaya for generations they are not quite Chinese either. They are only Straits Chinese. (It is true, of course, that there are now considerable numbers of Chinese in Malaya who came from China and are trying to make a lot of money as quickly as possible before returning to the motherland. It is also true that more and more of these change their minds and stay on.) The Straits Chinese are, on the whole, determined to prove two things: (*a*) that they are true Malayans; (*b*) that they are true Chinese. These aims are neither contradictory, nor are they dishonest: Malaya is, after all, their home but their culture is Chinese and they have every right to be proud of it. China is a distant and often unknown land for them and she certainly looks more attractive and alluring from Selangor or Penang than she does from the vicinity of Hong Kong. The emigré's relationship to his country of origin is a complex one. I know it only too well; I have been a Straits Hungarian long enough.

Retail trade and all the professions are almost exclusively in the hands of the Chinese. The Malays do not really resent this. Nor do they hold it against the peaceful Chinese

citizens that terrorism used to be entirely a Chinese affair.
What they do resent is the feeling that many Chinese look
down on them, which many of the Chinese indeed do, some
on intellectual grounds, others because 'we pay all the taxes
here'. Not that the Straits Chinese are such scrupulous and
zealous tax-payers as all that. Malaya is the only country
in the world where there are more automobiles than income-
tax payers.

* * *

The fears and forebodings of the English were not justified.
They are not persecuted or made uncomfortable in the least.
The Malays are not only charming but also sensible people.
They often tell their English friends: 'Without your help we
could not have achieved all this.' And they mean it.

The English, for their part, were quick to forget the old
days of the white *tuan*. It can still happen sometimes that an
Englishman gives two different parties to different sets of
friends – but he does that sometimes in London, too.

The English are needed in Malaya at the moment. Many
have been dismissed from their Federal Government jobs
and re-engaged by the Malayan Government for the same
post at higher salaries. Also, they were given a large lump
sum in compensation for 'loss of employment'. The English
have always been a tolerant people; they do not mind this
at all.

Yes, far from there being tension, there is racial peace in
Malaya – unlike Singapore. The roles are neatly cast and
each race is prepared to play his allotted part. The races do
not compete, they complement one another. They live side
by side; they cannot live really together. Chinese and Malays
cannot eat together (as most Chinese dishes contain pork)
and they cannot drink together (because the Malays must
not drink). So they can hardly mix even if they wanted to.
In any case, the main reason for this peaceful co-existence

is the common-sense, tolerance, wisdom and easy-going philosophy of the Malays. They are a proud people and devout Moslems but somehow all the dark, dogmatic and fanatical traits identified in some countries with Islam have just melted in their hands as Buddhism melted in Siam. Islam in Malaya has become mild, attractive and even smiling. Well, why not? In some country even Christianity is Christian.

THE NEW MONARCH

Malaya, on becoming independent, decided on a monarchical constitution. The various Malayan states were formerly ruled by Sultans and one of these was now elected paramount ruler, the King of Malaya.

The honour fell to the Sultan of Negri Sembilan, Abdul Rahman. Malaya, by the way, is the only country in the world where the King and the Prime Minister have the same name. To make the matter even more complicated, both Abdul Rahmans are princes, *Tunku* or *Tuanku* in Malay. The election of Tuanku Abdul Rahman ibni-l-marhum, Tuanku Muhammad, K.C.M.G., caused some surprise. He was only third in seniority among the Sultans. But his two seniors, the aged and celebrated Sultan of Johore and the Sultan of Pahang could not be elected for very different reasons.

The Sultan of Johore, Major-General Sir Ibrahim, D.K., S.P.M.J., G.C.M.G., G.B.E. (Mil.), G.C.O.C., (1) is eighty-five years old and has been on his throne for sixty-three years. But it was not his old age, although this was pleaded as an official excuse, that prevented him from becoming king. He simply did not want the job. In the early stages he even objected to Malayan independence and thought that his country ought to maintain a closer tie with Britain, although his was the last Malay state to accept a British adviser. The

Sultan of Johore is a strange mixture of great ruler and fabulous, old tyrant and he is not exactly enthusiastic about 'more power for the people'. His resistance to Malayan independence was eventually broken but he still refused to become King himself, and though his former hostility has by now mellowed into nothing more than a stern frown, he still does not really approve of the new state. And in any case, he wants to spend most of his time in London, not in Kuala Lumpur.

The Sultan of Pahang, Sir Abu Baker Ri' had to be discreetly passed over for a different reason. He had married one wife too many: five, instead of the permitted, desirable and moral four. In addition, the fifth wife used to be a cabaret singer which would have endeared her to my heart but I had no say in the matter. Sir Abu is a light-hearted and easy-going gentleman, extremely popular and much loved in his own state. But he could not become King of Malaya because he did, undeniably, over-marry.

Tuanku Abdul Rahman, the new King, is sixty-three years old. He was called to the Bar in England and is a member of the Inner Temple. He became a barrister in 1928 and became Sultan – or to be more precise, not Sultan but Yang di-Pertuan Besar, which means something like His Highness the Greatest Gentleman – in 1933. He came to England to attend the Coronation in 1937 and has been here on several occasions since. Tuanku Abdul Rahman now lives in Kuala Lumpur, having severed his connections with Negri Sembilan. His son acts as Regent for him.

The Malayan monarchy presents two curious features:

1. It is not a hereditary monarchy. When King Abdul Rahman dies, his fellow-Sultans will elect his successor from their own ranks. The King of Malaya is an elected monarch, as the rulers of the Holy Roman Empire were between the thirteenth and nineteenth centuries.

2. Many people believe that, paradoxically, the establish-

ment of the monarchy will lead to its extinction in Malaya.
The argument is that the existence of the paramount ruler
will lead to the decline, waning and final disappearance of
the individual Sultans; then, in turn, the extinction of the
individual Sultanates will lead to the decline and final
extinction of the monarchy.

DEATH AND MAH-JONG

It is always interesting to observe how other people live; in
Malaya it is equally interesting to observe how other people
die. You cannot sojourn very long in the country without
noticing the Death House.

The Death House is a Chinese institution. People are sent
there to die because the Chinese regard it as bad luck if
people die at home. Yet the Death House seems to be a
fairly gay place on the whole. I watched the one in Johore
Bahru for a long time. Relations were sitting at little tables
outside the house chatting and playing mah-jong. They are
in the habit of playing on till late in the night – I was told –
and the rattle of the mah-jong bricks rather disturbs the
nocturnal peace of the neighbourhood. The gaiety is neither
irreverent nor is it impious: all Chinese funerals are gay,
the colour worn for mourning is white and death is regarded
as something of a practical joke on God's part. I fully agree
with the Chinese. Why should leaving this world be any
sadder than entering it? Death is, after all, in a way more
natural than birth. All people die; but the great majority
of us are never born. Death is no tragedy; only a frustrated
and spoilt life is.

So the relations wait outside and the honoured father,
grandmother or whoever the person may be, waits inside.
The patient inside is always more impatient than those outside, because he cannot play mah-jong. What a person feels
when he is hastily dispatched into the Death House, I

cannot say. Nor can I say, for that matter, what a person may feel – not in Malaya but in England – on being taken through a doorway bearing the inscription in huge letters, HOSPITAL FOR INCURABLE DISEASES.

Malays have no Death Houses of their own. They eat at home; they live at home; they die at home.

'A Malay, often a well-educated Malay at that,' a Malay friend of mine told me, 'will call in the doctor if he is ill. If the doctor is of no help, he will call a witch-doctor. He doesn't believe in him, of course; but just in case. The chemist, by the way, will be Chinese. In most Chinese chemists' shops you can see magic herbs as well as penicillin and bicarbonate of soda. But he won't go to hospital because if he is to die he wants to die at home. A Malay must be really on his last legs to agree to be taken into hospital.'

'Isn't that rather illogical?' I asked.

'Why illogical?'

'If someone has nothing seriously wrong with him he has no reason for not going to hospital. But if one is mortally ill and wants to die at home, surely, he ought to stay at home.'

My friend fell silent for a minute.

'I never thought of that,' he said at last. 'And never shall. One only goes to hospital in case of mortal danger. Because one wants to die at home. That is the way it is.'

THE DOG

But for me Malaya was first of all Somerset Maugham country. Mysterious, luscious, violent. I was prepared to see murders and lonely suicides and I expected people to draw me aside after the third whisky and soda and tell me about long-forgotten homicides they had committed. When I was informed at a party that a certain planter was a widower I stuck to his company full of expectation that he would tell me how he had killed his wife and explain all about those footprints in the jungle. The fact is I never heard a good murder story. People either refused to confide in me as freely as they used to confide in Mr Maugham or the planters are committing fewer murders than in a bygone and happier era.

The planter – so it seemed to me – is hard-working, ambitious, hospitable and usually quite well off. He dislikes artificial rubber and loves whisky. There is nothing romantic about him. He leads a good but not luxurious life. He has, as a rule, plenty of servants.

I found the story of Malayan rubber more interesting than most of the planters I met. Malaya got rich on good luck – at least, as far as her income from rubber is concerned. Tin is also produced but there is nothing extraordinary about Malayan tin. Tin has been mined by man for 4,000 years and Malaya herself was a known tin-exporter in the ninth century. Rubber is an altogether different story. The Director of the Singapore Gardens, Henry Nicholas Ridley, suggested in 1888 that South-American rubber trees should be imported via Kew Gardens and planted in Malaya. The idea was laughed at and strongly resisted. But Ridley was adamant and when in 1911 he retired, as an old-age pensioner of modest means, Malaya was already one of the world's most important rubber-producing countries. And yet the Marxists go on talking of 'historical inevitability'. If Corsica had not been attached to France (as Bertrand Russell has pointed out) and Napoleon Bonaparte had been born an Italian citizen, the history of Western Europe would have been very different; and if the Director of the Singapore Gardens had been a less stubborn man and had insisted with less obstinacy on what seemed an idiotic whim, Malaya might not be today a rich and independent country.

* * *

Done in 1077 –
Ridley greatly improved production and was knighted about 1911 – he moved to Kew + lived to over 100!

Tracing Mr Maugham's own footsteps, I went to The Dog
—the famous Selangor Club. It is a very pleasant place. Its
Indian porter is one of the most magnificent figures I have
ever seen. Food is good; drinks are cheap; conversation is
as spirited as in any London club (which is qualified praise);
and the hospitality of members is lavish. I asked the Russian-
born secretary whether the Club was still exclusive.

'Very exclusive indeed,' he replied. 'But if you mean
racially exclusive, well, then we are not.'

'You have Asian members?'

'Plenty of them. Asians are welcome.'

I asked for, and obtained, permission to take some film
at lunch-time next day for b.b.c. television. My crew of
cameramen and other technicians arrived on time; I was
having a drink with some members at the bar, waiting for
more people to arrive. I saw no Asians at all.

'They don't very often come for lunch. You'll find more
Asians at dinner-time.'

'What a pity,' I said. 'You see, it makes an enormous
difference to the viewer whether I show them Asians and
Europeans mixing happily together or whether I tell them:
"There are plenty of Asian members in this Club. They
don't happen to be here just now but honestly, you may
take my word for it." '

While this argument was going on, two young Indian
ladies came in. Both wore red saris; both had the Hindu
religious sign on their foreheads; and both were exquisitely
beautiful. The secretary introduced me to them – one name
sounded to me like Mrs Sakhrayana; the other lady was
Miss Something.

I asked permission to sit at their table and be filmed in
their company. Mrs Sakhrayana kindly agreed. We chatted
while the cameras and reflectors were being fixed up and –
let it be stated in all fairness – quite a few other Asians
arrived in the meantime.

'But you are not English,' said Mrs Sakhrayana, noticing my foreign accent.

'No. I'm only British. I'm really Hungarian.'

'So am I,' said Mrs Sakhrayana, the beautiful Asian member of the Kuala Lumpur Club in the red sari and with the Hindu sign on her forehead. 'I come from Vienna. My maiden name was Heft.'

SIAM

CONFESSIONS OF A CRYPTO-SIAMESE

It would be almost impossible, I thought, for Bangkok to live up to its reputation. I heard so much while I was in Asia about the delights of the Siamese capital and the charms of its people that I was almost biassed against them before I arrived. What can Bangkok have to offer – I asked myself with a frown – to a man who has seen Hong Kong? Can the Siamese be more likeable than the Malayans?

But Bangkok and the Siamese did live up to their reputation, if not quite in the way my informants meant. Bangkok is not a beautiful city, in fact, it is a very ugly one. It has no shape or plan; it is almost as confusing as London without London's many redeeming features. The gods are housed all right but human beings are less fortunate. In other words, while the temples of Siam, especially the Temple of the Emerald Buddha, rival in magnificence European architecture at its best, there are less than half a dozen decent buildings for mortal habitation and there are far too many ramshackle huts and other eye-sores. The city is a strange

mixture of oriental splendour and oriental filth. But if the
Malayans never stop smiling, the Siamese never stop laughing. Even their currency unit has the delightful name of
tical, pronounced tickle.

I could not help falling in love with their philosophy of
life, which had, in fact, been mine for a long time. I had
been a crypto-Siamese without being aware of it. It is the
philosophy of the shrug of the shoulders – not, however, in
a cynical 'couldn't care less' manner. On the contrary. They
accept the pleasures of life gratefully but certainly not avidly.
But why worry? Why hurry? Things are never as important
as they seem. And, hurry or no, we shall all arrive at the
same destination sooner or later. Is the earth's existence
really threatened by the hydrogen bomb? Most regrettable
if it is indeed so, but why worry before it blows up? After
all, it may never happen.

Ambition, advancement, prestige and keeping up with
the Siamese equivalent of the Joneses are notions as strange,
indeed, incomprehensible, to the Siamese as the idea of
being happy and content in a primitive mud hut (without
hot water and the usual offices) would be for a New York
salesman.

Siam – or Thailand, if we want to be pedantic – is the
only country in South-East Asia which has never been under
the domination of any European power. She was, however,
occupied by the Japanese during World War II. The
Japanese tried to treat the Siamese as brethren and fellow-
Asians, flattered them in many ways and even added
territories to Siam at the expense of her neighbours. But
foreign occupation cannot ever be made really enjoyable
and few Siamese were sorry to see the Japanese depart. Siam
is also the only country in South-East Asia which was not
compelled to fight a Communist uprising after the war.

The Government is nevertheless harassed by a Communist Party, whose members are mostly of Chinese race,

and a large number of fellow travellers, mostly Siamese intellectuals. Most trouble has, however, been caused not by Siamese but by Malayan Communists who infiltrated from the jungles of Malaya into the jungles of Siam where they maintain their headquarters to this day.

Not to have been under European domination is partly a blessing; but it is also a little annoying. The Siamese have always been free men and this may well be the explanation for the pleasant and open manners of the Thais – although I know quite a number of European races which have always been free, yet are far less pleasant than the Siamese. They treat Europeans as their equals, do not know what a 'white sahib' complex is and have no feeling of inferiority on account of their colour (which, by the way, is a much more attractive colour than ours and ought to give them a superiority complex, if anything). After the war, there was a terrific upsurge of Asian nationalism. All the peoples of this region fought glorious battles for their independence, got rid of their European masters and proved that they could manage their own affairs. But Siam could fight no glorious battles for her independence because she was independent to start with; she could not get rid of her European masters because there were none. She found no way of proving that she could run her own affairs, having already proved that long ago to everyone's satisfaction. She had her own civil service, army, navy, and air force; and even her civil airline, with Siamese aircrews. The whole of South-East Asia was in a ferment, drunk with the exhilaration of a dream come true; and poor Siam felt a little bit left out of it.

This situation had to be remedied in one way or another. And with the help of the Communists and their fellow-travellers, as well as that of the naïve nationalists, it has, indeed, been remedied to some extent. If anti-European feelings did not exist after the war, they could, with a little effort, be created; if there were not too many Europeans

E

about to serve for a proper target, more and more Americans were pouring in to serve on SEATO – and the establishment of the South-East Asian Treaty Organisation gave, of course, a new impetus to the Communists in this campaign of denigration.

In the last two years or so, there has been an irresponsible campaign in the Thai press against all Europeans. It is not too violent – nothing the Siamese do is too violent. When a half-drunk American sergeant got into a brawl with some Siamese in a night-club over a Thai lady of easy virtue, huge headlines in some of the papers next morning complained about the womanhood of Thailand being insulted by imperialists. Or if a big American car knocked down a poor – and preferably old – Siamese pedestrian, these papers clamoured about 'The Way They Treat Us!' This kind of thing has been going on for quite a time, week after week, if not day after day and it has made some impression. Many Europeans feel extremely irritated and will tell you that Bangkok is not such a pleasant place to live in as it used to be. But it is, as I have said, still pleasant enough. Some Europeans are too sensitive; after all, over-sensitiveness is not an Asian monopoly. And, all things considered, the Siamese do not really care; because, after all, nothing really matters anyway.

ON FILMS AND CONCUBINES

In Siam everybody is called by his or her Christian name (or Buddhist name – anyway, I mean the first name) exactly as on I.T.V. People's family names are usually unknown even to their friends. If your name is, say, Bisdar Siwasariyanon, everyone will call you Bisdar. The letters you receive will be addressed to Bisdar – your surname will not be put on them. Your servants will call you Mr Bisdar. If you meet

people on equal terms they will call you Bisdar. And even
when you become really intimate with a person, he will not
start calling you Siwasariyanon.

The trishaws – the tricycle taxis – are great fun. They are
not quite as uncomfortable as some European taxis but they
are already quite as expensive. Neither taxis nor trishaws
have meters and the visitor is well advised to settle the
question of the fare before he starts on his journey. I, personally, do not mind being treated like a tourist and I do
not complain when cheated. But the cheating should contain an element of decency and moderation. On one occasion
a taxi-driver demanded thirty *ticals* for a journey I wanted
to make. I offered him fifteen but he refused and muttered
something about me in fluent Siamese. I stopped another
taxi and offered the driver ten *ticals* which he accepted with
thanks. As I had paid seven *ticals* for the same journey the
day before, I began to wonder whether, in fact, even five
ticals would not have been overpaying him.

*　*　*

Siam is prosperous; the Siamese are poor. The country is
about twice as large as Great Britain and has about one-
third of the population. Although wages and incomes are
very low, even the poorest man in the country lives high
above starvation level. 'There is rice in the field and there
is fish in the pond' they say and they are content. They are,
indeed, very conservative within the sphere of their own
contentment, they do not hanker after improvement and
desire no change. They marry the two or three women they
love and live with them happily ever after.

The Siamese may, in fact, marry one woman only but
they may keep as many concubines as they can afford. The
various ladies are, however, kept apart so that the Siamese
male has to maintain several separate households. Their

system is more or less the same as in many European
countries except that it is a little more moral than ours
because it is all above board involving no furtiveness or
lying. None the less, a Siamese may sometimes lie to his wife
and tell her that he has been with one of his concubines –
which is right and proper – while he was, in fact, gambling
– which is wrong and immoral.

Many families are now westernised but apart from these,
Siamese wives are kept very much in the background. They
seem to be humble and silent servants but in reality they
very often hold the purse-strings and keep their lords and
masters under their thumbs. Eighty per cent of all the real
estate in Siam is said to be in the hands of women. The
women are shrewder and more sensible in business matters
than the men, who tend to be spendthrifts and gamblers.
As one Siamese man told me with endearing sincerity: 'We
are all right as a race because our women are so wonderful.
They have all the virtues of our race; we have all its vices.'

*   *   *

In the matter of lowering film production costs the world
could do worse than take a lead from Siam. Since printing
is too expensive, the Siamese make only one single, silent
copy of each film. Since Siamese films are very popular in
the country, more popular than any foreign film, the single
copy is literally played to shreds. An actor and an actress
attend the cinema during the performances and speak all
the parts, male and female, over a loudspeaker system. They
have a wide variety of different voices at their command.
Animal sounds, when needed, are fairly shared between
them. Foreign films are dubbed into Siamese in the same
way. *Around the World in Eighty Days* was the only recent film
to be given a gala performance: no less than three actors –
two men and one woman – were present.

HOW TO ORGANISE REVOLUTIONS

The Siamese have three great national institutions in which they firmly believe: (1) their religion; (2) their national revolutions; (3) their monarchy. A close look at each of these will help us to understand the Siamese character, which is neither oriental nor inscrutable.

The national religion of Siam is Buddhism and the King is the Defender of the Faith. It is widely held that it was this undogmatic and attractive religion that created the pleasant Siamese character. The truth is exactly the reverse: it was the pleasant Siamese character which turned their own version of Buddhism into such an attractive and undogmatic creed, so different from, for example, the cruel rigidity and dogmatism of Tibetan Buddhism. Religion has, of course, a great effect on peoples; but national character has an even greater counter-effect on religion. Islam, too, has been mellowed in Malaya, just as Christianity has often been commercialised in the United States or as a Protestant version of Catholicism has been invented in the Land of Compromise.

There are 18,416 temples and monasteries in Siam and the images of Buddha far out-number the human population. For more than thirteen centuries all the artists of Siam have produced these images and practically nothing else. The images are made of all sorts of materials and vary in size from minatures to the 378-foot giant at Nakorn Pathom. But otherwise they differ little. Siamese artists cannot be accused of seeking originality at all costs. They have been patiently copying the same images for 1,300 years and they would be rather shocked and apologetic if it could be shown that any trace of originality had slipped into their work in the meantime.

You cannot walk ten minutes in Bangkok without meeting several monks in their yellow robes. Every young man has to become a monk at one time in his life. It is a kind of national service. There is no territorial army in Siam; there is a territorial priesthood. In the monasteries young men purify their minds, study the scriptures, learn self-denial and self-discipline. On entering the monasteries they have to give up all their worldly possessions – even the yellow robes do not belong to them. On the buses they are carried free of charge and on trains they pay half-fare but someone has to accompany them to the station and buy their tickets for them because they are not supposed to have money even for half-fares. That is why I was somewhat puzzled when I saw a young monk buy a lottery ticket in the street. Lottery tickets may be the exception. I cannot really tell.

Very early every morning hosts of monks are to be seen begging for their food. But the 'mendicant friar' is a purely European notion and what the Siamese monks do is, in fact, not begging at all. They walk from house to house giving people a chance to acquire merit and grace by filling their bowls with rice, boiled eggs, omelettes, fried fish, etc. They do not ask for anything nor do they thank you for what you give. They must not utter a word. Indeed, it is for *you* to thank *them*: it is you who have acquired merit through their services.

(Another way of acquiring merit is to free birds. You can buy caged birds in front of the larger temples, open their cages and set them free. I had the vague feeling that someone must have previously lost a little merit by catching these birds but, after all, it is always the sins of others that give us an opportunity of being virtuous.)

Most young men serve two, three or six months as monks. Initially they all join up for life. To become a temporary monk is unheard-of. It is quite in order to join for life and quit after a few months. The King himself served a stretch. He stayed in holy orders for fifteen days.

* * *

Revolutions are the second great national institution of the Siamese. Wars are out of fashion with these sensible people. In the past they had plenty of wars, mostly against the Burmese and sometimes the *casus belli* was provided by white elephants. But politics being what they are, these white elephants were really only red herrings.

The Siamese revolutions are, on the whole, pleasant affairs. They may be less world-shaking than the Russian Revolution but they are certainly much more comfortable to live through. Few people understand, however, exactly what happened in September, 1957, and why there was a revolution at all. Marshal Pibul Songgram himself did not quite understand it until it was too late.

Briefly the story is this: Siam was invaded and occupied by the Japanese immediately after the attack on Pearl Harbour. Nai Pridi – a hero of the 1932 revolution and a member of the Regency Council – thereupon entered into a secret understanding with the Allies and became the leader of the resistance movement, while Marshal Pibul Songgram – who led the army officers in 1932 – collaborated with the Japanese. After the war, Marshal Pibul and the collaborationist army officers suffered an eclipse and the liberal Nai Pridi formed a rather left-wing government. In June, 1946, King Ananda was shot dead in mysterious circumstances and in 1947 another of the periodical revolutions broke out: this time Marshal Pibul, notwithstanding his past, regained power and became, first, Commander-in-Chief of the army and later Prime Minister. Nai Pridi eventually fled to China, where he still lives and where he has been drawn nearer and nearer to Communism. As in Siam it was the army which usually helped various revolutionaries to success, certain opposition leaders thought it might be a good idea to obtain the help of the navy on their own behalf. In 1952 Marshal Pibul, however, humiliated and disarmed the navy, jailed many of Pridi's followers, received much American aid and went on ruling the country with little trouble until 1955.

To counterbalance the influence of the navy, Pibul built up another strong force – the police, always a pretty formidable factor in Siam. In command he placed Marshal Phao. His other right-hand man – and successor in the post of Commander-in-Chief of the army – was Marshal Sarit. Phao and Sarit were excellent choices. Pibul knew perfectly well that a dictator does not need 'strong men' to help him to maintain his grip; he needs weak men – and that is why these two marshals were chosen. In addition, he could play them off easily against one another. So Pibul was comfortably set for a nice peaceful rule but he committed two grave mistakes.

A dictator can afford to do many things. He may even conceivably do a great deal of good for his country. But a dictator must dictate. He may be feared; he may even be respected; but he is never loved. The dictator who tries to become a constitutional ruler and starts hankering after the love of the masses, digs his own grave. And that is exactly what Marshal Pibul Songgram did.

In 1955 Pibul – for the first time in some thirty years – left his country. His journey was not really necessary. He came to Europe and, among other countries, visited England. He had a good look at the House of Commons, at the Opposition and at our press and – amazing as it sounds – he liked it all. During his tour Pibul conceived the idea of becoming a democratic leader – indeed, a freely elected, democratic leader. On his return to Siam, he allowed opposition parties to form, he tolerated an opposition press and decided to hold elections.

We do not need to follow all the intricacies of Siamese politics to understand how Marshal Pibul came to grief. But it was not really the expected and foreseeable that followed – Pibul knew better than that. He won his election all right and where results were not sufficiently presentable,

Marshal Phao and his police saw to it that they were sub-
jected to some secret plastic surgery. Pibul, in the end, was
not defeated by the opposition he had created; he was
thrown out by his own friends. And he was not even dismissed for political reasons. His successors and former
associates continued his former policies, which are right-
wing, strongly anti-Communist and, while very much in
favour of American aid, not very much in favour of
Americans.

What happened, then? Pibul's two right-hand men had
both built up formidable business empires. One controlled
the lotteries and a few banks, the other controlled all the
trade with Red China. Both enjoyed innumerable other
monopolies, among them – and no doubt without their personal knowledge – the opium trade and the brothel industry.
Both men also controlled a number of newspapers and the
whole game became so complicated that sometimes the two
Marshals were attacked in their own papers. The ensuing
revolution in September, 1957, was simply the clash of
business interests. Politics hardly entered into it. Marshal
Pibul was out and had to flee the country before he, the old
fox, could realise what it was all about. No one was really
against him. But it had to be either Phao or Sarit, and Pibul
was not a business ally of either.

Marshal Pibul did not leave the country as a poor man.
Once it came to a clash, Sarit was bound to win, simply
because he was Commander-in-Chief of the army and the
army was still much stronger than Phao's police. Not that
these respective strengths were ever measured in deadly
combat. One single round was fired in the Siamese revolution by a startled sentry in the outskirts of Bangkok. No one
was hurt.

THE KING AND I

Siam is as deeply and sincerely royalist as England. King Bhumibol Adulyadej is thirty-one years old and he is the younger brother of King Ananda, assassinated in 1946. He is married and has three daughters.

It is extremely difficult to have an audience with the King, as he is very carefully protected. But if he is rarely seen, he is often heard. He is often heard because he is the composer of popular light music. His music is frequently performed by various Siamese orchestras and sometimes even in the United States where, however, it is not quite so warmly acclaimed as in Siam. The King's other great hobby is photography and his pictures are sometimes reproduced in the press. King Bhumibol is a retiring young man. He likes best – I was told – the 'company of his fellow musicians'.

In spite of all the caution of his courtiers, the King often drives about in his own fast sports car. Few people recognise him in the street: the Siamese are not very observant and the royal car has no special royal number plates. The King likes speeding but up to now he has had no trouble with the police.

Court etiquette is very strict and formal. The feet and the head still play an important part in Siam. It is held that a servant's head must never be higher than his master's and a subject's head must never be higher than the King's. To think of a servant's or a subject's *feet* being higher than the master's or the King's *head* is almost sacrilegious. That is why until recently high houses were not allowed to be built in Siam, in case people's feet should be higher than the sovereign's head. (The building of brick houses was not allowed either. Only royal palaces and temples could be built of brick.)

Today these restrictions have been eased but are still strictly adhered to in the presence of the King himself.

Royal pages, for example, have to crawl on the floor in the royal presence.

To crawl properly, pages and servants need acrobatic skill. At least one palm has to be flat on the floor which the servant's forehead must also touch. If, in addition, he has to carry a large tray with, say, thirty-two filled glasses on it, his performance becomes a virtuoso act worthy of any circus. This crawling is still the rule in the houses of some aristocrats, too, but it is getting rarer and rarer and a growing and intelligent new generation is trying to abolish it as quickly as possible. Yet, the old habits die hard. A prince of the royal blood – a charming and enlightened young man – said to me: 'I abolished the practice in my own house long ago. Or, rather, tried to abolish it. I told my servants that worms crawled – not human beings.'

'They were delighted and grateful?' I remarked.

'Not so much delighted and grateful as upset and very resentful,' he replied. 'They are very conservative. They believe in my being a prince and their being servants. They like crawling, too. They say they owe me some respect. I tell them I don't quite see why but that in any case, they must find some other means of expressing their deep respect for me and give up crawling.'

'So they gave it up?' I said. 'With regret, maybe, but they gave it up.'

'Not at all. They are still trying to get away with it. They crawl less but they still crawl as much as they safely can. They walk up to me with a tray and then, when handing me a drink, they suddenly collapse. They crawl when they think I don't see them, too. And the amount of crawling that goes on as soon as I am out of the house is almost incredible. In Europe little children start crawling on their own and as soon as they are able to crawl they are taught how to walk; in my household little children as soon as they can walk are taught to crawl. My servants love crawling. They seem to enjoy it. They also believe in it and regard it as their birthright.'

I understood. There is a strong and noble desire in the bosom of men to be free; and an equally strong and noble desire to remain a slave.

INDIA

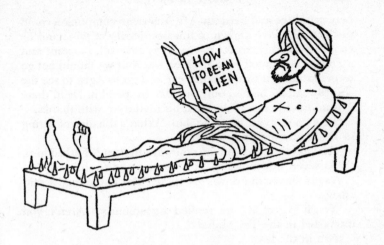

A DAY-DREAM

My plane developed some slight mechanical defect and was about three and a half hours late in taking off from Bangkok. Thus it was that I arrived at New Delhi at three o'clock in the morning instead of 11.30 p.m. As soon as I emerged from the plane the Indian authorities gave me about two dozen forms to complete, mostly in duplicate. I have never been in a country where the authorities provide you with so much clerical work as in India. It is a graphomaniac's paradise. I remember one of these forms with special affection: it had to be filled out in triplicate and in the end they told me I could keep all three copies. All the officials were, however, polite and efficient, so once I had finished my homework, I was allowed to proceed without further delay.

An American gentleman invited me to share his car into town. I readily agreed. I am of a friendly disposition and prepared to chat with almost everybody at any time, except

between three and five a.m. My American companion could
not possibly have known of this peculiarity of mine and he
could reasonably expect me to be as cheerful, buoyant and
matey as he himself was. His idea was that we should not go
to bed at all but hire another car and go to Agra to see the
Taj Mahal. As he had only one day to spend in Delhi there
was no time to lose. I declined his invitation with thanks.

'Be a good sport, bud,' he said. 'What's the idea of sitting
in Delhi wasting your time?'

'At what time did you say you want to start?' I asked him.

'At seven this morning. It'll be nice and fresh.'

A cold shiver ran down my spine. 'I'm not going,' I said
curtly.

'You'll regret it,' he replied melodiously. 'Aren't you
interested in the Taj Mahal?'

'Not in the least.'

He was perplexed by this answer. After some reflection,
however, he volunteered this statement: 'I've always been
interested in the Taj Mahal.'

I murmured some reply, half asleep.

'Even as a kid,' he continued chattily, 'I can't say why,
but I was just nuts about the Taj Mahal.'

'Where do you come from?'

'Seattle, Washington.'

'And in Seattle, Washington, as a kid you were just nuts
about the Taj Mahal?'

'Yeah!' Then he added: 'Guess I'm nuts about people,
too.'

I looked at him with surprise and he went on:

'I don't know what it is in people that gets me. But I'm
nuts about people.'

'There must be something in them,' I suggested.

'Yeah. My wife, she thinks the same. Sometimes my wife
and myself go out just to meet people. For no other reason –
just to meet people. Ordinary guys, mind you.'

'In Seattle, Washington?' I asked.
'Yeah.'

*   *   *

Perhaps my companion from Seattle lacked the wit of an
Alexander Woolcott, the charm of a Gary Cooper and the
felicity of phrase of a Thurber, but in a few days I was driven
to the conclusion that I was doing exactly what he had
suggested.

I, too, went to see the Taj Mahal in the end and went
about just meeting people – ordinary guys, mind you. I
failed to rediscover India and early enough gave up any
hope of so doing. I satisfied myself with checking up on
some of my preconceived notions of India and sensing its
air. I cannot even attempt to describe India; I can only
describe my own short visit to India.

I must add that India was about the only place in Asia
I did not want to see. I had long nourished a deep antagonism
towards India – for which India herself was hardly responsible. When I was a child in Siklos in Hungary, my
grandmother – whom we children called Mother Rosa –
often came to see us from Budapest. Mother Rosa was a
poetic, lofty and sublime soul. She was fond of using long
Latin and Greek words – usually incorrectly – and she loved
to close her eyes and recite sentimental poetry in a half-
whisper. She often told me, with a wistful sigh, that her most
ardent wish in life was to see India. Would I, too, like to see
India? I said that I would not. She tried to coax me. She
closed her eyes and whispered of the strange beauty and
unfathomable mysteries of India. But I remained adamant;
I still preferred to stay at Siklos. We children made fun of
our grandmother's lofty flights of fancy and her poetic
manners and I decided at the age of six that I would avoid
India and, should I be unable to do so, I would not be
impressed.

But my grandmother was right and I was wrong. I wish she had succeeded in persuading me to go earlier. India is one of the most fascinating and inspiring places in the world. I expected to find morose, grim and fierce nationalists (as visiting Indians here, feeling as they do always on the defensive, often are); I found instead a polite, good-humoured and hospitable society. But touchy they certainly are. And here, India may fulfil a long-cherished dream of mine.

In my early youth I often pictured myself as a brave and defiant satirist. It was my hope that my various writings would create an angry storm which I might face with a supercilious smile on my lips, with unflinching courage and unshakable defiance. But no storm ever came. I awaited an outburst after the publication of *How to be an Alien* but the English patted me on the back and absolutely refused to get annoyed. I fared better with my next book on the Americans: they wanted motherly love even from me and treated me with a certain lofty disdain. But lofty disdain was not enough: I wanted a storm, just a little abuse, a tiny bit of fiery indignation. That, alas, was denied to me. I attacked – or thought I had attacked – various countries in turn and they all nodded beaming approval. It is true that I was challenged to a duel by an angry young patriot from Pisa because of my book on Italy. I was preparing to fight him at five o'clock one autumn morning in St James's Park. The heavy cavalry sabres were ready and the television cameras were getting into position when my challenger sent a message to say that now he had *read* my book, he found it not only inoffensive but, in fact, complimentary to the Italians, wherefore he was calling the duel off and offering me his lifelong friendship. In my little book on Israel I was rather rude to some Arabs. At a diplomatic reception not long afterwards an Arab Ambassador walked up to me and asked me sternly:

'Are you the author of that book on Israel?'

'I am,' I replied, full of happy anticipation. 'At last, it's coming,' I thought jubilantly. But all the Arab Ambassador said was:

'You ought to come to *my* country and write a book about it. It's much funnier than Israel.'

Now, India is my last remaining hope. I have been warned many times and by many people that the touchiness of the Indians is unlimited. They want praise and admiration from everyone and take all criticism – well meant or otherwise – as an insult. I hope this is true.

A lifelong hope and ambition will wither away if it is not. How I should love to see myself facing 370 million Indians and sticking to every word I wrote. Any angry outburst would be appreciated. And an attempt on my life . . . oh, well, let's not indulge in day-dreams!

TWO HOLY MEN

I got up at eleven o'clock or so on the day of my arrival and at once sallied forth to see New Delhi. Hardly had I left my hotel when an elderly gentleman – a Sikh, with an impressive white beard – accosted me: could he read my future? I said I did not want to know my future and started to walk on. Little did I know Sikh fortune-tellers; before I could make it any plainer that I was not interested in his services, he was busily engaged in reading my future and my past. He began by giving me a piece of thread which he told me to break into five pieces. I obeyed his instructions, whereupon he crumpled the thread up in his hand and then gave it back to me: it was all in one piece. I was duly impressed and was about to walk on when he asked me whether I would give him two rupees for telling me really amazing things about myself – such as no other fortune-teller in the whole world could. I accepted his offer. Almost at once he asked for two more rupees. I handed them over, rather hoping they might remind him that I had already paid him. He asked me to follow him to an empty site because – he explained – we needed privacy. There, behind a fence, lurked another Sikh gentleman who was later to be introduced to me as his assistant. The fortune-teller took a piece of paper and a pencil from his pocket, wrote something down and informed me that he had made a note of the year, month and day of my birth. Then he put the paper back in his pocket and started to talk of other subjects. A few minutes later he asked me (just to check up, as he put it) when exactly I was born. I told him; but he must have been caught many times by practical jokers because he asked me repeatedly whether I had given him the right date. I assured him I had – which was the truth. After several further digressions he, at last, produced the bit of paper from his pocket, showed it to me and, sure enough, there was the date of my birth recorded on it. (After a considerable amount of hard thought I was able to reconstruct how this was done. When he first said he had written the date down, he had merely scribbled something. Later when he asked me to verify the date, his assistant hidden behind the fence, wrote down what I said – and this is why the magician was so concerned to know whether I was speaking the truth – and passed the bit of paper on to him unobserved.)

After this successful display of his magic powers, he asked for his fee. I reminded him that he had received it twice. He waxed indignant. Those four rupees had been a voluntary contribution for good luck; surely I would not refuse to pay him his fee, on which we had agreed? No, I certainly could not do anything so mean and un-English, so I handed him two more rupees. He produced another piece of paper and announced that he was setting down my wife's Christian name. Soon he asked me casually what her name was and shortly afterwards – exactly like the first time – he produced the right name. He proceeded to work the same miracle with the names of my children. Suddenly he seized my right (or was it the left?) hand, studied the palm, and broke into loud thanksgiving. I was, it appeared, going to receive £30,000 before Christmas. The money is overdue, I must admit, but it was not overdue at the time of his prophecy and I could not really refuse him another rupee in return for a promise of £30,000. Almost before I knew where I was – certainly before I knew where his assistant was – I had given him fourteen rupees – more than £1.

He told me to beware of a girl called Mary which I have done ever since. He wrote down my profession and I told him I was an agent for refrigerators. A few minutes later he produced the inevitable piece of paper from his pocket on which he had put down with magic insight that I was an agent for refrigerators. After some consultation with his assistant he asked for another two rupees.

'No more.' I shook my head sadly.

'Two rupees,' he said coolly and firmly.

'No!' I said more coolly and more firmly.

'One?' he suggested.

'Nothing.'

'Half?'

'Nothing.'

He paused. I had proved an almost inexhaustible source of supply, the type of mug every Sikh fortune-teller dreams of and now I had suddenly grown stubborn. There was more pain than anger in his voice:

'It's not the money. Money is nothing to me. But it would break the spell of your luck if you refused.'

'The spell will be broken,' I replied. 'It's a pity, but broken it will be.'

'Listen,' he said in even sadder accents, 'you cannot refuse. It is impossible. I am a Holy Man. If you do not give me another two rupees you will break a Holy Man's heart.

Surely, you are not willing to break a Holy Man's heart for the sake of two rupees?'

'It grieves me deeply,' I answered. 'But I find myself in a serious dilemma. You see, I, too, am a Holy Man. And if I give you another penny, it will break *my* heart.'

His eyes twinkled.

'Thirty thousand pounds is a great deal of money,' he declared solemnly. 'You will have it before Christmas.'

'Will it be tax free?' I asked but he dismissed this important point without taking any notice of it.

'Will you give me a hundred when you get the money?'

'I'll give you two hundred,' said I. 'Give me your name and address.'

I rather suspected that his name and address were the last things he was prepared to give me but I was curious to see how he would get out of it.

'Fear not,' he replied with a superior, almost holy smile. 'I shall find you wherever you may be. I shall not fail to claim my share. I am a Holy Man.'

'That's settled, then,' I nodded.

'Can you give me two rupees' advance?'

'No.'

'One?'

'No.'

'Half?'

'No. You'll have your money as soon as I have mine.'

'Money,' he exclaimed contemptuously. 'You Europeans keep talking of money. You are such materialists . . . Believe me, young man: money is not important.'

BULLOCK CARTS AND JETS

India has given me some severe shocks.

The country's recent history seems to prove the pernicious

theory that it is possible for people to behave in a simple, sane, commonsense manner. What is to become of our world, I have asked myself on several occasions, if India's bad example is followed and more and more peoples and governments start acting like normal, human beings? The consequences would be incalculable. Such an ominous trend would endanger the existence of governments and the United Nations and might shake the very foundations of civilisation.

A grave responsibility for all this danger rests on British shoulders. They started it. Whoever had ever heard, prior to 1947, of an Imperial Power giving away its most valuable possessions of its own accord? And – to make matters worse – giving them away without any strings attached? Many people pointed out that, after the withdrawal of the British, India's elementary duty was to collapse in chaos. And, indeed, much terrible and unforgivable bloodshed followed both in India and Pakistan, yet order emerged from the chaos and this – many people declared, shaking their heads in grave disapproval – is against all the laws of history. India ought to have broken up into small fragments; the Princes ought to have created unsurmountable difficulties; the country ought to have gone bankrupt through inefficiency and corruption. It was only by a defiant breach of the laws of history that India refused to do all these things. It was impossible – the prophets went on – to co-ordinate the bullock cart with the jet plane. Yet, the Indians have made some progress even in this field.

And whoever heard of trying to establish a democracy in Asia? India ought to have become an ugly tyranny. Did not many people foretell with visionary fervour and prove with unanswerable arguments that India was not ripe for democracy? If she was not ripe, it was very bad taste indeed to try the experiment. An unripe democracy, I gather, is a terrible thing; far worse than a beautiful, ripe totalitarian tyranny. And now we are confronted with this totally unripe

democracy in India which has the further effrontery to work
reasonably well.

A lot of thoughtful Indians (and in no country, not even
France, have I met so many thoughtful people, passionately
interested in world affairs) throw nervous glances in the
direction of China. China is not only India's great rival for
Asian supremacy, she is also a possible model. (Japan, the
third contender for Asian hegemony, is conveniently classified as a non-Asian power, just as England used to be
regarded as non-European; European or not, Britain more
or less ran Europe for a century.) China, as the Indians
cannot help observing, is able to deal with all her problems quickly and energetically unhampered by the clumsy
dilatoriness of the democracies. While there are a large
number of fellow travellers in India, Communism has, too,
many undisguised apologists. Would it not be possible to
take over some traits of the economic system and copy the
steady progress of China without importing the ugly features
of Communism, too? A tempting thought. But they go on
sticking to their democracy under their great leader. It is,
I warn you, sheer commonsense.

Many of China's achievements, it should be added here,
are not due to her go-ahead and ruthless totalitarian system
but simply to the diligence and perseverance of her people.
And that is something the Indians could scarcely take over,
the truth being that quite irrespective of their political
systems the Chinese are more hard-working and also thriftier
than the Indians.

Another deplorable example of sheer commonsense at
work is the case of Kerala. This southern Indian state has
decided, by democratic franchise, to go Communist. Kerala
is, in fact, the first state in the world where the Communists
have come to power by democratic means. Political scientists
will no doubt write learned tracts in analysis of the Kerala
experiment but even the most unscientific observer must

clearly realise the unenviable position of both sides in the Kerala affair. What is a democratic Central Government to do with a Communist state? What would the American administration do if California or Wisconsin suddenly – and I admit, somewhat unexpectedly – turned Communist? And again, how is a Communist government itself to behave with democratic overlords sitting on its neck? Whatever conclusions the theoreticians may arrive at, the position involves a most amusing battle of wits. The Central Government tries to get rid of the Communists by scrupulously legal methods; on the other hand, the Communists are determined to behave like little angels even if it hurts, in order to deprive the Central Government of its excuse for ousting them. The Central Government would not think of stooping to any doubtful methods; and the Communists – a minority government, by the way – behave in a rather un-Communist way, so as not to supply valid grounds for Government action. Once upon a time we witnessed – or so we were told – 'Socialism in one country'; now we can witness 'Co-existence in one country'.

I could go on with my charges against the Indians. You would expect, for example, a country that has struggled for independence for such a long time, to find itself frustrated and disappointed on achieving it. Such is human nature: fulfilment of a dream is normally the greatest anti-climax life has to offer. The end of the most romantic of love stories is, as a rule, that 'they went on being dreadfully bored by each other ever after until death them did part'. India, however, is an astonishing exception to this rule, too. The Indians are consciously happy with their independence. They are always prepared to learn on a trial and error basis; they are always happier when committing their own mistakes than when taking over the tailor-made, ready-to-wear wisdom of others.

This well-nigh inhuman degree of commonsense would,

if unrelieved, be most disheartening. Luckily, the Indians
do have their redeeming features of human weakness, vacilla-
tion and misjudgement. They show, for instance, much more
understanding towards Communism than towards the West.
It took Nehru a long time to see the real nature of the Russian
action in crushing the Hungarian Revolution of 1956. He
was forced by public opinion to change his apologetic attitude, although it should be added that he most probably
would have come to change it of his own accord. Even great
statesmen must take facts into account provided they shriek
loudly enough into their ears. The explanation of this curious
and constantly recurring attitude is very simple. The Indians
experienced British rule but never experienced Russian rule
– so they are apt to assume that the British danger is real
and the Russian purely imaginary, hardly more than a
bogey painted by the Western Imperialists to frighten the
poor Indians. In addition, castigating the British is an
ancient Indian tradition and not all the harsh words are
really meant to be taken too seriously.

The other field where Nehru and his government have
their blind spot and behave like the rest of us, is the Kashmir
question. Here the wise arbitrator rejects arbitration; the
staunch upholder of the United Nations will not hear of the
United Nations; the apostle of the democratic principle will
not hear of a plebiscite; as soon as the word *Kashmir* is
uttered the calm philosopher becomes semi-hysterical and
the reasoned tones of the Wise Old Man become shrill
and malevolent. Nehru may or may not be right on this
issue: but he is adamant. He is not adamant because he is
right; nor is he adamant because he is wrong: he is adamant
because he himself is a Kashmiri. A few Indians told me in
confidence: 'We are not so up in arms about Kashmir as you
might think. But Nehru is. We owe a great deal to Nehru
and love him dearly. That's why we all act as if Kashmir
were a matter of life and death to us. But it isn't.'

I do not know how widespread this attitude is. But it sounds convincing and human – simply because it is hypocritical and unethical. The Indians are all right, I sighed at last, on hearing this; we all are brothers.

HOW ENGLISH CAN YOU GET?

It is in the noblest English tradition that India is resisting with all her might the importation – nay, the imposition – of the decimal system. The Government has reformed the currency on the decimal basis and has introduced the metric system but the population resists these reforms gallantly. The decimal system is easy to understand and logical to handle and therefore quite unacceptable to any nation which has basked for so long in the noblest English traditions.

In some English ways the Indians surpass the English. Indian muddle is in many respects not only worthy of, but superior to, the muddle of the ex-mother country. It takes an average Continental visitor of normal intelligence from eight to eighteen months to master the English monetary system. The Indian system was until recently different though no simpler: 16 annas used to make a rupee and 12 pies (or 4 pice) made an anna. But this was not muddling enough for the legislators so they resorted to the idea of simplification. Simplification causes an incredible amount of further muddle. At present they have both the old and a new system running parallel, the latter involving a new division of the rupee into a hundred *naye paise* (new pice). You get your change in a mixture of old and new money. Most people do not bother to check it at all, taking it for granted that they have been given the wrong change in any case. But this dual system is quite simple, in fact extremely easy to handle if you keep in mind that 1 naya paisa is 1.92 pies, 5 naye paise are 9.6 pies, and that 4 annas and 3 pies make 27 naye paise.

If you really want to get on without difficulty in Indian business life you had better remember that 1 candy is 560 lb. in Bombay but only 500 lb. in Madras, while 1 lb. is 0.454 kilograms both in Bombay and Madras. And you must not forget that 1 tank is equivalent to 68.1 grains (in Bombay alone) which makes 72 tanks, as you have no doubt already noticed, exactly 1 seer. Not more, not less.

A major legacy of the English is, however, the weather-mania of the Indians. Why Indians should say, 'Lovely morning, isn't it?' in a country where almost all mornings are only too lovely is not quite clear. Maybe only extremists greet each other in this way. But they are all frantically interested in the weather, in weather reports and forecasts. When the government introduced the clear and simple centigrade system – which, however, no one understood in India – and newspapers started giving temperatures in centi-grade, their circulation fell tremendously. So now the degrees Fahrenheit are added in brackets and the lost flock is returning.

Partial or total prohibition and the problem of pub hours provide another wonderful field for keeping up the tradition of British Imperial (now Commonwealth) muddle. Here, too, the Indians have greatly improved on the Mother Country. The right to regulate these questions was left to the individual states and they have all regulated them differently 'in accordance with local conditions and circum-stances'. In some states you may buy drinks for consumption at home but you may not consume them in public; you may not drink in the bar of an hotel (to make the solution of this problem somewhat easier hotels have no bars) but you may drink any amount in your own hotel room; you may drink in clubs except on certain days. (Why it is more sinful to drink on a Tuesday than on a Wednesday, is not quite clear to me, but I am not really at home in the mysteries of India.) Certain other states – Bombay and Madras among them –

have ordered total prohibition. But even in those states you may obtain a limited amount of spirits if you can produce a medical certificate to prove that you really need it. The result is that perfectly healthy and respectable people provide themselves with the required permit; and the majority of the British in Bombay are proud and happy in the possession of certificates proving that they are habitual drunkards and chronic alcoholics who could not survive without their daily dose of whisky.

There are no speakeasies and there is no bootlegging yet on the scale of the Chicago of the 'twenties, but a great deal of the forbidden juice is manufactured by peasants and smuggled in and out by professionals. Toddy (local distilled spirit) and rice-wine are the most popular commodities among the Indians and the smuggling of whisky is the best business for the European consumers.

Most people doubt whether these anti-alcohol laws are a real success. I am sure they are. I feel certain that their purpose was not to prevent alcoholism (in which they have failed) but to maintain a fair proportion of the traditional British muddle (in which they have succeeded gloriously).

How English is India on a deeper and more significant plane? I do not know the answer but it is clear that 300 years of close association did not pass without leaving many deep impressions. The most English remark, in more senses than one, that I heard in India was made by a literary gentleman who was, moreover, unaware that he was saying anything extraordinary:

'I am working on a long essay on Kipling. The result will be a complete revaluation of Kipling. He has not only been misjudged in these parts of the world but also definitely under-rated.'

Speaking once of a Scots friend of mine, an outstanding linguist, to a lady (and a well-educated lady at that), I mentioned that he knew something like fifty languages. The lady started counting on her fingers and after prolonged calculation, she declared:

'Nonsense. There aren't fifty languages in the world.'

'You haven't forgotten Schwitzerdeutsch?' I asked anxiously.

'Certainly not,' she replied coolly.

I have already mentioned the seventy languages of the Philippine Islands but these are a mere trifle. The 1951 census enumerated a total of 845 languages in India. Even if this figure includes a number of dialects, India's linguistic problems look pretty formidable. The Constitution recognises fourteen of these as 'the languages of India'. English is not one of these. But Sanskrit (mostly encountered nowadays in temples and old manuscripts and 'spoken' – according to the official statistics – by one thousand persons) *is*. The living Indian languages vary greatly in currency and prevalence; the largest group of languages (Hindustani) accounts for almost half the population – 46.3 per cent, to be precise – while Kashmiri, the smallest of the recognised living tongues is used by a fraction of one per cent. Languages whose very existence is unknown to the majority of people outside India, such as Gujarati, is spoken by more people than Hungarian and Czech put together and even Assamese – who has ever heard of Assamese? – is spoken by more people than Norwegian, the language which produced an Ibsen and a Björnson.

The language question of India is partly an administrative and partly, perhaps largely, a nationalistic problem. The nationalistic aspect of the problem takes two different forms: an Indian language – as the future national language of India – versus English; and the various Indian languages versus one another.

The Constitution decided that 'Hindi in the Devanagari script' should become the country's official language in 'not more than fifteen years' – i.e. by 1965. The Devanagari or Sanskrit script was chosen because Hindi when written in the Arabic (or near-Arabic) script is nothing else than Urdu, the national language of West Pakistan. Urdu has absorbed many Persian and Arabic words and is not quite identical with Hindi; but – roughly speaking – it is only the way of writing which divides these two languages. So we have Urdu-speaking and Hindi-speaking people who can understand each other's words but cannot – even if literate – read each other's scripts; and farther east we have the Chinese and Japanese who are more or less able to read each other's scripts but do not understand one word of each other's spoken language.

Hindi, Urdu and Punjabi (the three used to be called Hindustani and they *together* make up the group spoken by the 46.3 per cent) are Sanskrit-type languages. Another 87 million people speak other Indo-European languages and can understand or at least learn Hindi without much difficulty in the same way as a Spaniard, for example, can learn French. Notwithstanding this similarity, people in the Punjab are not any keener to exchange their own language for Hindi than the Spaniards would be to give up Spanish and adopt French. But to complicate the issue considerably, a further 88,000,000 people speak Dravidian languages and to a Telugu or a Tamil, Hindi is as much a foreign language as English. Hence many people are against the compulsory teaching of Hindi. Sometimes they protest mildly; sometimes they protest vehemently; occasionally they riot and kill a few people here and there. But never too many.

This linguistic imperialism of Hindi is, to a great extent, well meant. Few people realise that one's relation to one's mother tongue is not much less complicated than one's relation to one's mother. English may be a world language and for dozens of reasons much more advantageous to know than Assamese or Oriya, nevertheless, it is only natural that the new India should have accepted English as a vehicular language only for a limited period. The governmental universality of English reminds people of the colonial days. Besides, a unified nation desires a unified language; and it is natural that the most extensive of the country's languages should be chosen for this role although Hindi cannot claim by any stretch of the imagination to be anything more than the most widespread regional tongue. In Israel, also, one can observe the unsuccessful discarding of English and the successful resurrection of a dead tongue; in Ireland, too, we may witness the same experiment even if a less successful version of it; and the mediæval Church resurrected Latin, though Latin was never really quite dead. But India's problems are very different from those of the mediæval Church and also from those of Israel and Ireland. Not only because India is at least twenty-five times larger than Israel and Ireland put together but also because in Israel and Ireland what is being revived is a dead *national* language while in India one *regional* group is aspiring to the dignity of national language at the expense of the others. English linguistic imperialism was all right in a sense – after all, what should one expect from imperialists but imperialism? The British were only doing their job. But making Hindi the national language is quite a different kettle of fish.

Objection to it is of course being rationalised. People point out the poor cultural heritage of Hindi compared with the riches of Bengali and Tamil. Then the non-Hindi speaking regions protest against their being degraded to 'second-class citizenship'. If Hindi is accepted as the language of the Central Government, and of higher education, they say, then those whose mother tongue it is, will have an

unfair advantage over the non-Hindi speaking population.
But this is, as I have said, mere rationalisation; the objec-
tions really cut deeper. The Indians may take it from me:
one cannot really exchange one's mother language any more
than one can exchange one's mother. The linguistic patch-
work of Central Europe is complicated enough although not
half as complicated as that of India. Yet, I have seen
Serbian-speaking islands in a Hungarian linguistic sea, German villages among Croats, Slovaks among Rumanians and
Hungarians among Poles. They have all lived in isolation
for centuries but they have all kept their mother tongues.
Young men may learn the foreign words of command in the
army but they certainly will be at a great disadvantage
when competing for government jobs or university scholarships. Hindi – however noble the original motives of its
sponsors – is out on a conquest; it is trying to snatch a
hegemony which is not its due. And yet the Indians have
no choice: they either have to deprive the other Indian
tongues of some of their rights or else they have to deprive
India of the hope of a more or less common language other
than English. But languages do survive and the future of
Oriya and Kashmiri and even of English in India, as well
as that of the other 840-odd languages, is not in danger.
People will go on speaking their mother tongues whatever
the official language may be. India may appoint an official
language but she cannot hope to create a universal national
tongue.

THE POT AND THE KETTLE

If there is anything the world dislikes in the Indians and in
their great leader, it is their tendency to sermonise. I have
already mentioned one example – that of Kashmir – in which
Mr Nehru recommends one set of rules to others and follows
another set himself. What of other fields?

F

The Indians were perfectly justified, of course, in struggling against British colonialism. Colonialism is wrong, they say. But is colonialism the only wrong? The oppression of brown men by white men may be wrong; but is the oppression of brown men by brown men right? Is the oppression of brown women by brown men so praiseworthy? And is the oppression of white men by white men (for example, Russian colonialism in the Soviet Union's East European Empire) really not worth talking about?

*   *   *

It is a grave mistake to believe that there is no racial intolerance or even a colour bar in India. Certain Negro student visitors to India whose story I heard in detail, had found it difficult or impossible to be invited to Indian homes and some had been virtually ostracised. The best I can say about this affair is that the Indians had, at least, the decency to be perturbed by it. They did say to themselves and others: 'But we cannot be colour-conscious; we cannot possibly have a colour bar. A colour bar here in India? Ridiculous!'

Still, if I were an Indian and I could have my choice, I should prefer to be of lighter than of darker colour. If a dark Indian wants to marry a really fair girl his chances are about as bright as those of a Texan Negro asking for the hand of a rancher's blonde daughter. There may be no real colour-prejudice in India but few people would deny the existence of a strong shade-prejudice.

How much of the caste-system has survived? Quite a lot. Caste is a real and ugly reality and an essential part of Hindu life. The Constitution guarantees equal civil and political rights to all citizens and the Government is certainly doing its very best to enforce the Constitution and – among other laudable projects – improve the lot of the untouchables. But the untouchables – the *harijans* – are still not regarded as human beings; they still would not dare to go to a village temple or take part in many more essential communal activities; a village barber would not cut the hair of an untouchable whatever the courts may say: he is readier to pay a fine than to lose all his customers; servants belonging to the lowest castes might speak to untouchables working with them but would not shake hands or share a meal with them. And you cannot force things in India. An English lady told me that soon after her arrival in Bombay she broke a vase and asked one of her eleven servants to sweep up the debris. But she apparently asked one who did not do sweeping, so he refused. So did the second; so did the third. Whereupon the lady lost her temper and, to set a shining example, picked up the broom and dustpan herself and swept up the broken glass. The servants looked on in silence. Next morning she rang in vain for the head-boy – and for all the others. All her eleven servants had left during the night: they would not stay in a house where the lady sweeps the floor.

The functional barriers created by the caste system are, in fact, breaking down very slowly; but, it is still impossible for a man to break out of his caste, be he a brahmin, a warrior, a tradesman or a peasant. Indeed, it is almost impossible even to break out of one's sub-caste – and there are several hundreds of these. Where one is born, one stays. No Hindu can eat with anyone outside his caste; no Hindu can marry outside his caste. An untouchable is condemned to untouchability for life – whether he is criminal or genius. Some untouchables become Sikhs or Muslims to escape from their castes, others simply move into the large cities – but there is no real escape from it. An untouchable may become a waiter in, say, Madras, as no one will trouble about a waiter's identity in a large city restaurant; but should he intend to marry he will have to marry an untouchable woman.

Caste system and democracy are strange bedfellows; they

cannot intermarry any more than a brahmin and *harijan*. The caste system induces you to see value in some people but no value whatsoever in others; your judgement will depend solely on the person's caste. You may remain utterly indifferent seeing a man dying in a ditch if he is a man of a low caste or an outcast. Foreigners and Muslims do not belong to any caste either – so they are of no real consequence.

This system vaguely reminds one of England. There are significant differences, however. In India, sacred cows and semi-sacred monkeys have their special position, but animals in general have no caste so people are, if not really cruel, certainly callous and indifferent to them. Animals in India can even be untouchables; in the caste system of England they precede the brahmins.

I pondered these questions deeply. How can a sincere hatred of colonialism and love of democracy be harmonised with acceptance or at least tolerance of the caste system – as it apparently can. Or is it simply the struggle of an enlightened government against backward masses? Is it simply the struggle of progress against Asian mediævalism? Seeking information, I discussed this with a Hindu friend.

'Most of the time,' I told him, 'I am more impressed by India than almost any other country I have ever seen. But sometimes I tend to think that you have a double set of values and that many of you are hypocrites. And that includes you, too.'

'Why?'

'Here in India you pose as a deeply religious Hindu. In England I watched you eating a steak. Do you deny it?'

'Oh, no. I don't deny it. You have certainly seen me eating steak.'

'Well – that's my whole point,' said I. 'Is the cow a sacred animal or not?'

'You don't understand. Hinduism is a great religion but the religion of India only. Indian cows are sacred; your

wretched English cows are not. That's why I don't eat steak
in India and that's why I eat it in England. I like it under-
done, by the way.'

At last I understood.

A secret of India – nay, a secret of the whole world, lay
suddenly disclosed before my eyes.

Our own cows are always sacred; wretched foreign cows
never are.

MOLARBAND

On our way to the village of Molarband, the Professor and
I drove through a number of other villages. Some of these
were really impressive, modern communities. The Indian
Five-Year Plans are achieving great results. The Indians
tackle their gravest problems in a brave and go-ahead
manner and produce results even if they cannot produce
miracles. The successes of their communal development projects are – in the words of an official pamphlet – 'substantial
but not startling'. India is doing much more for herself than
the British ever did for her in the field of community development but they know perfectly well that even their greatest
achievements have just scratched the surface of poverty.

From our jeep we could see squalid and putrid villages
some distance off the road, but all round new and almost
attractive little huts were going up. We saw a gang of men
doing heavy road-work with pick-axe and shovel.

'These men belong to one small tribe,' the Professor
explained. 'They undertake certain work communally. There
are plenty of these tribes about. Their wages are paid to the
headman. Very miserable wages they are, but the workmen get only half even of them. The rest is pocketed by the
headman.'

'And people accept this situation?' I asked.

'There is nothing they can do about it. But even if they
could, they wouldn't. They accept everything here.'

'I often wonder,' I said to the Professor, 'how these people, who accept everything, can show themselves so intolerant on occasion.'

'You are wrong,' he replied. 'They are never intolerant. Sometimes they go berserk. They massacred Muslims when they were being massacred by the Muslims. A "mad career of violence" – as Gandhi put it – is always a possibility here, but these people are never really intolerant. They often sulk; they withdraw into their shells; they reject you – but they are not intolerant.'

Our jeep left the road and followed a track; then the track ceased, too, and we went on over the fields. I saw some animals in the distance. At first I thought they were huge dogs but soon realised they were cows. Thin, miserable, underfed cows: the sacred animals of India. The village when we reached it was full of mud and filth, squalor and stench. All the huts were built of mud, too, and yet it was different from what I had expected. Communal filth ran together with at least some attempt at personal cleanliness. I do not mean that the people squatting in the mud in their filthy loin-cloths and other nondescript rags were themselves clean; I only mean that the interiors of these huts, in spite of their muddy floors and foul atmosphere, were considerably cleaner than their exteriors. As the average annual income of an Indian is put at £18 (and the word *average*, of course, implies that many earn less), one can expect neither running hot water nor too many modern gadgets in the kitchens. But the children were well fed and looked healthy. Four or five small children were running around stark naked. Under a tree I saw a tiny, beautiful baby fast asleep. There were so many flies buzzing round and on him that I thought they might eat him up completely.

In the Welfare Centre of Molarband about twenty-five children were being looked after by kind women. We went to see the school, too. About a hundred children between the ages of six and eleven were squatting on the floor; some of them were doing sums, others were reading torn and ragged books. There were a hundred children in the whole school, which comprised five different forms. Education is not compulsory and it is a sacrifice on the parents' part to send a child to school instead of having him to help around the house. There was one girl to ninety-nine boys. One little boy had his left eye nearly eaten out by trachoma.

In the street again I saw many women carrying incredibly heavy burdens on their heads. This gives them their wonderful carriage, I had often been told. I should like to have seen them carrying less even if they walked perhaps a little less graciously. These women work from five in the morning till eight at night. They are all slaves but not one of them would marry under her subcaste.

We passed two or three dung-hills and reached the quarters of the untouchables. I found the same mud huts, the same filth, the same stench. No better, but certainly no worse than in the other parts. The position of the untouchables has greatly improved in the last two decades. Their children are at school. No high-caste child would shake hands with them or share a meal with them; but as children do not shake hands with anyone in any case and as there are no school meals in India, this is only a minor drawback. The village folk might speak to them and they might even be allowed to take part in community meetings. Untouchable women may go to the village well but may not draw water. They have to wait till some other woman draws it for them. They are thus spared the work but have the water.

'This is not a poor village,' the Professor remarked. 'It's reasonably well off as villages go. There is no starvation here. There is little starvation in the north but a great deal of it in the south.'

'There is a fine distinction,' said I, 'between famine and starvation. Famine is rapid death, starvation is slow. The world could hardly afford another Indian famine; but it can afford starvation.'

'And it does afford it,' the Professor replied.

I asked him what he thought was the largest single factor in India's poverty.

'The lack of desire to improve their lot. They are not content, of course, but they are resigned to their fate. Reality is accepted. The disease of America is the mad desire of everyone to "get on"; the disease of India is the complete absence of this American disease.'

'What about over-population?' I asked.

'Birth control is gaining some ground. Very, very slowly. But the trouble is that this village has only two radio sets. One belongs to a "rich" peasant, the other to the community.'

This sounded pretty incoherent to me.

'We were talking of over-population, Professor,' I said politely.

'That's what I'm talking about still,' he answered. 'To solve India's over-population problem we need more radio sets, more cinemas and the introduction of television. And millions of television sets as soon as possible.'

I looked at him in puzzled surprise. He explained:

'Over-population! You see, there is just no other amusement in these villages.'

*   *   *

From the untouchables' quarter we went to another and more distant part of the village where the snake-charmers lived. Only a few were at home: most of them were busy in Delhi, charming snakes. We went into a hut, sat down and asked the men to charm a snake or two for us. So one of them squatted down on the floor and started to play an alluring Indian love song on his flute. An old man with a white beard brought some baskets; a number of children stood round us. Slowly one of the baskets opened and the

ugly head of a cobra reared up. Then another cobra from
another basket. Then a third. In no time the whole tent
was teeming with poisonous cobras which crawled towards
us only to be picked up by a little boy of four or five and
handed over to the chief snake-charmer who went on blowing the flute. The snakes crawled about – sidled up and
down nervously, so to speak – but refused to be charmed.
The man went on blowing his flute, playing his plaintive
love song and shaking his body. Its effect was irresistible on
the Professor, our driver and myself. We stared at the man
hypnotised, and slowly started to rock rhythmically from
side to side. Soon we were all thoroughly charmed, except
the snakes. Finally, he gave up.

'These snakes are very young,' the Professor interpreted
what the snake-charmers had just explained to him. 'They
will have to be trained.'

As I was leaving the tent, the largest cobra hissed at me
furiously.

'Beginner,' I hissed back contemptuously and walked out.

THE MAHARAJAS

In the old days one used to hear a great deal about the
fabulous riches of India; nowadays one hears almost exclusively of her fabulous poverty. But India is rich, even if the
Indians are poor.

The former Maharajas, once among the richest Indians
(*maha*, by the way = great, *rajah* = prince), were often in
my thoughts while I was in India. How were they doing?
Were they still able to make ends meet or were they out of
a job? Was there anything I could do for them?

The first two bits of information I gathered about them
put my mind more or less at rest. One Rajah, it appeared,
was still living in his old palace but had had to cut down the

number of his servants to 250. Possibly my face did not show
enough sympathy on receiving this piece of intelligence, as
my informant added:

'And that includes outdoor staff, too.'

That shook me. I had not imagined that the 250 could
include outdoor servants, too. Another Maharajah, fed up
with an India which could get on without him, emigrated
to Ethiopia. Finding there that he needed some farm-
labourers, he had 3,000 Indians dispatched from the home-
land. The rest of his employees are Ethiopians.

About one-third of India was princely territory. There
were 565 Maharajahs, all told (including Rajahs, Nizams,
Nawabs, etc.). Their territories ranged from 10 to 84,000
square miles. While they were all sovereign rulers, they had
accepted, however, the suzerainty of the British Crown.
British snobbery with its titles, distinctions in speech and
its 3,600 subcastes compared with India's 360 is a pretty
formidable institution; but it fades into insignificance compared with this bygone, princely world. Imagine the fun in
England if every duke, every baronet, every knight-bachelor
were entitled to the correct artillery salute wherever he
might appear. Imagine the cannonade in the city every
morning, in Clubland at lunch-time and in the night-clubs
after dark. Imagine the embittered squabbling over the
number of guns one is entitled to. Studying the changing
pattern of England I feel certain there would exist by now
a National Union of Peers with an efficient though im-
poverished marquis as its general secretary. There would
be general excitement all over Britain once a year when the
N.U.P. came out with a fresh crop of demands. Is it possible there would be strikes, too, for a yearly increase in
salvoes due?

When Britain quitted India, the princes were left without
their protector. Some of them argue that Britain broke her
word and let them down, since no time limit was set to their

treaties with her, which were thus to be valid indefinitely.
Whatever the rights or wrongs of this argument, I should
perhaps point out that 565 British-protected principalities
scattered over the new state of India would be rather a
strange arrangement even by British standards. Besides, as
long as Britain had an army in India, she could protect these
widely-scattered feudal or semi-feudal rulers, but how could
she protect them when her army, even at Aldershot, is
decreasing rapidly? Or are we to infer that England should
never have left India but should have stayed there to protect
the princes?

The rajahs were advised to come to terms with the new
republic and they accepted this advice. Only two – the ruler
of Kashmir and the Nizam of Hyderabad – caused any great
difficulty. The Nizam, after protracted negotiations, decided
to declare his country's independence. In September, 1948,
Indian troops invaded Hyderabad but after a four-day
'police action' the Nizam changed his mind. He became
rajpramukh – appointed democratic governor – of his own
state and all has gone well ever since. The Nizam is a great
old gentleman and still one of the richest men in the world.
In Kashmir, a Hindu prince ruled a Muslim majority
and the troubles created there are far from over yet. The
new Indian state, in turn, behaved generously with the
maharajahs. They were allowed to keep their titles – by far
the most important thing to them – and receive diminished
but still huge allowances for their privy purse – which is not
unimportant, either. Their allowances cost a pretty rupee
and are the subject of a great deal of criticism but it has
been said, and rightly, that this was a small price to pay for
a bloodless revolution.

Many of the maharajahs still live in their old palaces, but
quite a few in reduced splendour. Some went to live in the
big cities, particularly Bombay; others again are in the diplomatic service and work efficiently and conscientiously; a

number have become constitutional governors like the Nizam of Hyderabad. Since 1947 about sixty princes have died. Their sons have, of course, inherited their titles and their pensions but several of them have decided to work for their living and have entered various professions. There are alto-gether twenty-six M.P.'s among the former princes. In England, I believe, almost all of them would be Socialists; in India none is.

TAJ MAHAL

Years ago I visited Rome but had no time to see St Peter's; later, the same year, I visited Athens and missed the Acropolis. When I arrived in New Delhi, all my friends told me that I simply must not miss the Taj Mahal in Agra. I hesitated. There were still many people I wanted to see in Delhi and I rather resented giving a full day to Agra. But my friends assured me repeatedly that this was the most magnificent building in the world. In the end, I gave in. I sighed, boarded the train and went to Agra.

The Taj Mahal, if I may be quite frank, rather annoyed me. Of course, it is beautiful. It is impressive and monu-mental and yet manages at the same time to be graceful. It is certainly one of the wonders of the world, being in the same category as – although certainly not superior to – the Basilica of St Peter's in Rome or the Cathedral of Milan. But somehow it is a very upsetting thought that all this magnificence is a tomb. All the guide-books and all the guides explained repeatedly that 'it was a wonderful and immortal monument to conjugal love and fidelity'. I am sure Mumtaz Mahal deserved it. She bore her royal hus-band, Emperor Shahjahan, fourteen children in seventeen years, so I cannot quite see how she could ever have had time to be unfaithful to him, even if her virtues had been less shining and admirable than they, in fact, were. Still, I could not forget that in a country where the housing conditions of the living are far from satisfactory, 20,000 men worked for seventeen years to provide a palace for two of the dead. I know that all this happened 300 years ago; I also know that the labourers on the Taj Mahal led a better life and worked much less strenuously than those who laboured on the pyramids in Egypt. Still, I should like to see the living conditions of the living preferred to the living conditions of the dead.

But even if I found the Taj Mahal rather a bore, my visit to Agra was richly rewarding. I drove and walked through the old town – a place most tourists carefully avoid or pass through as quickly as they can – and was thrilled by every minute of it. The dust was hot and thick and full of the stench of sweating bodies; there was filth and poverty wherever you looked. There were people clad in wretched rags, sleeping on the pavements, in the gutters and in the dust. One man sitting near a dunghill was applying drops to his diseased eyes. And so on – an endless throng of sick and suffering men and women.

And yet I loved them. All of them. And it seemed to me that much was being done for them by their own government and that while India was huge and the Indians many, their lot would slowly improve. Almost immediately doubt assailed me: Can it be done? Is it not a hopeless battle?

While I was musing over these questions, I suddenly became aware of a group of people coming towards me almost at a run. I stepped aside to let them pass and saw that it was a funeral.

'They are burying an old woman,' the guide explained.

The dead woman was covered over with a thin cloth so thin that the outline of the corpse could clearly be seen. She must have been skin and bone as they were holding the stretcher high quite effortlessly. Another three or four men followed behind, chanting.

India is a very hot country. This old woman could not have been dead very long.

'What are they going to do with her?' I asked my guide.

I learnt that they would either burn her or bury her. 'Bury', of course, meant that they would throw her into a hole and cover her over with a thin layer of earth.

And then I suddenly remembered the Taj Mahal, the magnificent tomb of Mumtaz Mahal and her husband, the Emperor. What about this poor woman? Perhaps she, too, bore fourteen children to her husband in seventeen years? I am sure that she, too, must have been a paragon of conjugal love and fidelity. She had no choice.

TURKEY

COFFEE AND SPINACH

If Istanbul is one of the most beautiful cities in the world, it is also one of the least attractive; and if it is one of the most expensive, it is also one of the cheapest.

Istanbul's natural beauty is breath-taking – there is no other word for it. Watching the Bosphorus, or rather staring at it in dumb amazement, some may be reminded of the Bay of Naples or Hong Kong or Rio de Janeiro; but it is really unique. You see the deep blue water between green hills – Europe on one side and Asia on the other – the graceful minarets and domes of the innumerable mosques, the red-roofed white houses and the slow-moving, lazy white boats on the calm sea; then the myriads of tiny lights when darkness falls and . . . well, it is no good trying to describe it. It beggars description; it's better – believe it or not – than Cinerama. Take a taxi and drive along the whole length of the Bosphorus, twelve miles up to the Black Sea, and you have seen one of the glories of the earth. Istanbul has, no doubt, a great deal more to offer – but for me Istanbul is the Bosphorus.

Many of the tourists who pour in – they are mostly Americans – dislike the place. For many people the beauties of the Bosphorus and the Golden Horn are cancelled out by the lack of coffee, the poverty of the Istiklal Caddesi – Istanbul's somewhat provincial Fifth Avenue or Bond Street – and the second-rate quality of the night-clubs. No doubt Paris is a better place for champagne and nudes; as to shopping – well, that's a different problem. If you are a souvenir-hunter you will find Istanbul a wonderful place for souvenirs from Istanbul: much better than Paris. But if you want to buy a few daily necessities, as well you may, or simply to reload your camera with an ordinary roll of black-and-white film, you will be disappointed. You simply will not succeed. At best you will only be able to buy 'Hungarian Kodak' at murderous black-market prices. Cine-films are not to be had for love or money. Nor will you be able to get a cup of coffee in the whole of Turkey, except in the houses of diplomats and the very rich. Someone has pointed out to me that the political maturity of the Turks has been gloriously proved by the fact that they re-elected a government which had deprived them of coffee. Many people thought that the lack of coffee would be the undoing of the Democratic Party. The Turks, in fact, are prepared to face hardship bravely if not exactly cheerfully; they work hard and forgo all comforts without a murmur. But the complete absence of coffee has come to be regarded as a national disgrace by the people who made 'Turkish coffee' renowned all over the world. One day the head-waiter of my hotel whispered to me:

'Good news. We have coffee today.'

'Excellent,' I said. 'Bring me a cup.'

He hesitated.

'I'm not sure,' he said, 'that you'll like it.'

'Why? What's wrong with it?'

'Nothing really wrong with it,' the head-waiter replied thoughtfully, 'but it is made of spinach.'

Novel as the experience of having a cup of steaming spinach after my meal might have been, I decided to miss it.

GOOD HATERS

Turkey has no coffee because she has no foreign currency. And that brings me to the outrageous extremes of expensiveness and cheapness characteristic of the country. You'll find yourself a black marketeer in currency before you know where you are. I did, too. Travelling to Turkey from Asia I landed at Teheran on the way. Noticing the 'Foreign Exchange' kiosk at Teheran airport, I decided that it would be a good idea to have some Turkish money on my arrival, and accordingly changed a very small sum of sterling into Turkish pounds. Not until I was in Istanbul did I discover that I had received more than double the so-called tourist rate and more than four times the ordinary official rate – and even so I was slightly diddled by my Persian friend. I lived on that small sum of money for five days in a first-class hotel and spent lavishly. You simply cannot avoid living in luxury in Istanbul – nominally one of the most expensive cities in Europe – for pennies. All very fine but at the same time disturbing. It gives you a bad conscience. (You go on doing it, of course.) There is hardly any currency control and consequently Turkey enjoys almost no benefit at all from her prospering tourist trade. While you live like a former Pasha for almost nothing, the Turks cannot afford a cup of coffee they love so much. Inflation is simply stifling their economy. Prices are ten-fold compared with what they were before the war and have doubled since the beginning of 1953. In the last six months the cost of living has gone up

by another ten per cent and wages have always lagged far,
far behind. All this tragedy just helps to make your sojourn
in Istanbul cheaper and pleasanter. Well, I like a good steak;
but I like to enjoy it with a clear conscience.

*   *   *

The almost incredible financial incompetence of the Turks
is accompanied by an abundance of banks unparalleled anywhere in the world. You can see a few banks around Wall
Street or in the City of London but these are poor shows
compared with even the outskirts of Istanbul. The city is
simply littered with banks – there are more banks in Istanbul
than cafés in Vienna, espressos in London or ex-Prime
Ministers in Paris. The explanation? I don't know. A car-
toon which appeared while I was there may give a hint: a
man holding a bank-note in his hand remarks: 'I've found
a hundred piastres and don't quite know what to do with
it. Shall I have a good meal or open a bank?'

The Turks make reasonably efficient administrators,
sturdy peasants and, above all, magnificent soldiers. Business has always been looked down upon as an inferior
activity to be left to the Greeks, Levantines and Jews. A
hundred years ago, a Turkish observer described Constantinople as 'Greek in its cafés and grocers' shops, French
in its fashions, English in its coats, German in its beer-
houses, Italian and Spanish in its music, Turkish in its
watchmen and porters.' The situation has changed considerably and today we have a number of Turkish millionaires
who have made their money mostly on cotton and congre-
gate, with some exceptions, in Adana. They do not collect
Renoirs and Sisleys as yet and do not hang Picasso drawings
in the bathroom or lavatory. This period will, no doubt,
follow. At the moment they live in the somewhat primitive
age of Cadillac-collecting and their slogan is 'one Cadillac
for each member of the family, two for Dad'. Millionaires,

however, are only a minority. The majority of the population is poor, even very poor, but they do not starve and there is hardly any unemployment in the country.

The Turks are brave and sensible but an unsmiling people and rather grim. The Sea of Marmora and the Black Sea form part of the Mediterranean basin but there is no Mediterranean operetta atmosphere in Turkey. They are not 'picturesque'; they do not burst out in melodious song without provocation – indeed, not even on extreme provocation. They do not parade in folk costume. In fact, of their two most characteristic articles of apparel, the veil was strongly discouraged by Atatürk, while wearing the fez was made a criminal offence. The Turks are hospitable and generous; they are also very patriotic. A sense of humour is not among their outstanding national characteristics. They are, on the other hand, good haters. Every self-respecting Turk will tell you that he hates the Russians, the Greeks and the Arabs. Of the Armenians and the Jews he will speak with only moderate enthusiasm. As a nation they like the Germans most. Not only because with their militaristic traditions and strong sense of communal discipline they are often described as the Prussians of Asia Minor, but also for traditional reasons. At the end of the nineteenth century when the Sublime Porte was regarded by most powers as a tiresome and unnecessary appendix of Europe, Kaiser William II proved to be the only – if not unselfish – friend of the isolated and despised Sultan. In short, they are a sober, industrious, hard-working and martial people – a far cry from the Hawaiians.

They are not in the least interested in politics. When I was there, Turkey was the centre of a world crisis – or that was what Mr Kruschev repeatedly declared. The Turks could not care less. 'If this is a Turco-Syrian affair,' they said with a shrug of the shoulders, 'you just leave it to us and we'll settle the Syrians in twenty-four hours. And the

Egyptians, too, if they care to join in. But if it is a Russian plot, then it is the business of the United States.'

Nor did they show much greater interest in their own parliamentary elections. It is true that in the last few days there were demonstrations and small disturbances. But these are traditional – it did not really mean very much. There was hardly any sharp issue in the elections. The great difference between government and opposition was that one was in power, the other was not; and there was, apart from personalities, absolutely nothing to choose between the various opposition parties. The government was blamed for the inflation and – a major issue, too – for the lack of coffee. On the other hand, they could plead the success of a huge building programme and the absence of unemployment. Having held power for over seven years, the government was re-elected for another term.

Communism is no danger at all in Turkey – one of the very poor countries of Europe. (By the way, make no mistake about it: Turkey is in Europe. It is refreshing to see in this era of Asia-mania, a country that *means* to belong to Europe.) I heard scores of people explaining: 'Communism is bad, simply because it comes from Russia. The Turks reject all things Russian, no matter what they are. If industrial capitalism were the creed of Russia, Turkey would have gone Communist long ago.'

The only political question that interests them deeply is the problem of Cyprus. They do not want Cyprus to go Greek and not only for nationalistic reasons. The Turks realise that the EOKA movement is Communist-inspired and fear – in my view rightly – that should Cyprus go Greek it will sooner or later go Communist. A glance at the map explains what that would mean to Turkey's security. The Communists in Cyprus are using – the Turks believe – the Greek Orthodox Church as their ally, or rather their stooge. They are convinced that the Greek Orthodox Church is playing – quite unwittingly, of course – the Communist's game. On this the Turks are adamant; they will not tolerate the Union of Cyprus with Greece. Aloud they proclaim that Cyprus should be divided into Turkish and Greek autonomous regions. But privately, when not overheard, they whisper: 'Let it remain British. What's wrong with the British?'

BAZAARS AND HAREMS

The Turks are somewhat noisy. The ear-splitting screams, the loud despairing yells and anguished howls you keep hearing do not mean that someone is being drawn and quartered or roasted alive; it simply means that someone is offering fruit or vegetables for sale. It seems that all the wailing dervishes of Istanbul – having been driven out of business by Atatürk – turned into barrow-boys and street vendors and today, instead of howling once every hour from a minaret, they go on howling incessantly under your window.

* * *

There are plenty of other sights on which to dwell in Istanbul, in addition to the Bosphorus and the Golden Horn. Byzantium, and later Constantinople, was, after all, the pride of the civilised world for eleven centuries. Constantine the Great made it the capital of the Eastern Empire in the fourth century; it fell to the Turks in the fifteenth. The Turks changed the city's name and character. They destroyed its standing in the world but added a great deal to its beauty. (The name Istanbul – the Turks prefer this spelling to Istambul – is not a Turkish word, but bastard Greek, deriving from *Eis ten Polin*, that is to say *Into the City*. So the first syllable of the name is really a preposition, the second the definite article.)

I do not know how many mosques you can do per day; my personal capacity is a maximum of two. If you can take more or have plenty of time, there are many of them and most are worth seeing. The St Sophia mosque (nothing to do with a Saint called Sophia although originally it was a Christian cathedral), the Blue Mosque, the Sultan Ahmed Mosque, the Valde Mosque and many others, are all great monuments and truly beautiful buildings – some of them even more beautiful inside than they are from without. I missed many of them but that was my loss.

If you want to do some interesting shopping, go to the Covered Bazaar. It can be vastly interesting, though disappointing in one way, as it is so quiet and orderly, not at all like one's cherished picture of an oriental bazaar. All prices are strictly fixed in Turkey, even in the bazaars. Atatürk did not rid Turkey only of the veil, the fez, the Arabic alphabet and Islamic tyranny – he also rid her of bargaining. Turkey is, I believe, the only country in the world in which all goods for sale carry two price tags – one showing the retail price and the other what the shopkeeper himself paid for the goods: the difference must not exceed twenty-five per cent and in many cases it is less. The result is that while the elegant main shopping street in Istanbul rather resembles an oriental bazaar, the bazaar itself resembles Bond Street. It is as quiet as a mosque; no shouting; no jostling and fighting, no bargaining. The place – to my great disappointment – did not even smell. Inside the shops courteous and well-dressed assistants await their customers. Heavens! what have oriental bazaars come to! You can buy everything under the sun in the ninety-two streets of this huge bazaar, but gold articles are the main attraction; there is also jewellery of high craftsmanship, trinkets, ornaments, chains, slippers and carpets. An exciting place, in spite of its incredible dullness.

★ ★ ★

But the most exciting places of all are the Sultans' palaces
with the harems. The Kiosk of Bagdad, in the Old Seraglio,
is a place belonging to the world of the Thousand and One
Nights. To quote an expert description from a little pamphlet,
called *Turkey*: 'The Bagdad Kiosk, once a room for mascu-
line repose and conversation over coffee, is beautified by
some of the finest tile-work in the Near East, and as for the
harem, the Sultan's wives and concubines certainly lived in
idle luxury, even if they were prisoners of custom. There is
a little pool outside the harem, and on a promontory jutting
into it the Sultan used to seat himself on balmy days and
watch his women frolic about him naked in the water and
on the pool's edge . . . In the tulip gardens surrounding the
pool gay fiestas went on far into the night. To enliven the
scene wax candles were affixed to the back of tortoises and
the wick lighted. The tortoises lumbered about among the
flowers, irked, no doubt, by the burdens they were obliged
to carry, but making a fairy-like pattern of moving lights.'

The splendour of the Dolma Bahce Palace rivals anything
to be seen in the royal palaces of Europe. Here are several
of the world's largest chandeliers, a present from Czar
Nicholas II. Among other famous gifts from the rulers of
Europe is a table sent by Napoleon, with enamel insets of
all – well, let us say, many of the women in his life. There
they are, his mother, his sister Pauline Bonaparte, and
Josephine and Marie Louise, among others, in a charming
family group. You can also see the largest bed in the world,
one which Abdul Hamid II had built for a visit of the Kaiser.
As you stroll along to the harem you pass wonderful mosaics,
doors decorated with mother-of-pearl, imperial kaftans
and other garments, and imperial orders handwritten and
addressed to various Grand Viziers. The alabaster bathroom is more than a match for the most fanciful similar
creation of Hollywood.

The harem itself, on the first floor, is a dreary, over-

crowded, almost slummy place. No decent municipal
authority would today tolerate such living conditions. The
gold-and-white boudoir of the head wife (the lady who
succeeded in bearing the first acknowledged son) is impressive enough. But the rest of the harem bears no comparison.
The eunuchs' quarters and the 306 rooms for the Sultan's
wives (and concubines, as there were only four legal wives)
consisted of tiny little cells. As there were sometimes more
than 500 women in the harem, some had to share a cell.
The overcrowding became so bad on occasion that one of
the Sultans – just to alleviate housing conditions – had some
of the girls sewn up in sacks and thrown into the Bosphorus.
The Sultan himself never came to the harem. It was always
the ladies who were ordered to visit him. Occasionally there
were parades and inspections – many were called but only
one was chosen. During the night the Chief Eunuch stayed
behind a thin silk curtain in the immediate vicinity of the
imperial couple and took minutes of the proceedings. Times
and other details were of the utmost importance; there were
too many claimants, pretenders and would-be princes as
it was.

UNCLE TURKEY

One evening in Istanbul an English friend of mine rang me
up and asked me to have dinner with him. I accepted his
invitation with thanks. Then he cleared his throat, coughed,
hesitated and, at last, asked me whether I would mind if
he brought a friend of his along. 'He's a Turk,' he remarked.
I said I should be delighted; while I loved the English, I
added, in Istanbul I preferred to meet Turks.

'But he's a millionaire,' he confessed.

I frowned. All millionaires are suspect in my eye; but
after all even a millionaire may be human. We could give
him a chance.

'What does he sell?' I asked my friend.

'What do you mean?'

'How did he become a millionaire? On what?'

'How should I know?'

'Well,' said I, 'how long have you known him?'

'For seventeen years.'

At eight o'clock that evening I appeared in the famous Abdulla Restaurant and was introduced by my friend to an elderly gentleman of distinguished appearance.

'Mr Burdur wanted to meet you,' my friend explained, 'because he loves Hungarians.'

I asked Mr Burdur whether he had ever lived in Hungary. He nodded approval with shining eye and gave me a happy and wistful smile. I asked him whether he had lived in Budapest or in the country. In Budapest, he told me. To be precise: in Buda. After a short pause, he added:

'I spent two years in the military jail on the Margit Boulevard.'

He sighed. His sigh was full of yearning and happy reminiscence.

At first I thought he was joking. But he was completely serious. During the war he had given up his business – whatever that was – and volunteered to work for the Allies. His wartime activities were never any more clearly defined, as far as I was concerned, than his peacetime job, but his work took him to Budapest where he was arrested by the Hungarian counter-intelligence service and thrown into jail.

He spoke as if those years had been the happiest years of his life. He was known throughout the prison as Uncle Turkey and he helped so many people and their wives and mothers and brothers and brothers-in-law that even today he was receiving scores of grateful letters from all over Hungary. In prison he learnt a little bit of Hungarian and some kind of amateur philology became his main hobby.

Since Hungary was under Turkish rule for a century and

a half, many Turkish words were absorbed by Hungarian. Uncle Turkey was hunting for these words now. He had spotted about two hundred of them and was blissfully happy when I guessed the meaning of some of them.

'What do you think the Turkish word for barley, *arpa*, means?'

'Is it perhaps *arpa* in Hungarian?'

'And the word for plough, *eke*?'

'Perhaps *eke*?'

He was really impressed.

'D'you speak Turkish?' he asked me.

'No,' I replied modestly. 'I've just been guessing.'

He asked me another five or six dozen similar questions. As I did not want to spoil his evening I said at last I could not quite guess what the Turkish word for apple, *elmar*, could possibly mean.

'*Elmar . . . elmar . . .*' I repeated with a puzzled frown. 'No, I don't know. I give up. What is it?'

'*Alma!*' he shouted triumphantly. He was so delighted with our philological conversation that he asked me for lunch next day.

Uncle Turkey's magnificent villa overlooks the Bosphorus and is one of the finest private houses in Istanbul. You sink knee-deep in his carpets. There were lovely chandeliers, heavy silver salvers and wonderful paintings wherever you looked. Eight footmen served lunch. We consumed the magnificent repast in a great hurry, rather in the way one eats at a serve-yourself bar during a rush-hour lunch in the City. This was because Uncle Turkey was impatient to take me up to his study and show me his souvenirs of Hungary. First came a little prison account book, with every item filled in by the Hungarian prison authorities on his behalf. It opened with a credit of 200,000 Swiss francs. On the debit side I saw such items as (expressed in their English equivalent): shoe laces – 8d, apricots – 10d, sent to Mrs J. Kormos at the village of Gyoma, £1. He produced a rusty, shapeless metal plate which he apparently kept locked up in one of the drawers of his desk.

'I used this in prison,' he explained with shining eyes. Obviously, the metal plate was one of his most cherished souvenirs.

'Have you ever been in prison?' he asked me.

'No, I haven't,' I replied and blushed. I did not dare to look him in the eye.

'I have many friends, though, who spent many years in prison,' I added, perfectly aware that this was a feeble attempt at re-establishing myself in his estimation.

'But you haven't been in prison yourself?' he asked again. He tried to speak courteously but was obviously finding it difficult to hide his contempt. After a painful pause, he asked me (in French in which language we always spoke) what the Hungarian word for 'bull' was.

'*Bika*,' I replied.

He shook his head sadly.

'It's something utterly different in Turkish.'

I was a bitter disappointment after all. I had never been in jail; and the Hungarian word for 'bull' did not bear the faintest resemblance to the Turkish word for it.

We sat there in complete silence for a long time, each of us sunk in his own thoughts. I felt deep sympathy for him. Poor Uncle Turkey – I thought. He had to leave the idyllic happiness of a Hungarian military jail. A cruel fate forced him to go on living the life of a millionaire in Istanbul.

*   *   *

From Istanbul I flew eastward to Ankara and a few days later I had to say goodbye to Turkey and Asia. Asia is mysterious and magnificent; rich and poor; exciting and dull; fascinating and exasperating. It is fashionable to be an Asian nowadays. I wish I could be an Asian myself but this

has not been granted to me. So what can I do? I keep
thinking of my old friend and bear the misfortune of living
the pleasant, free life of an unrepentant European with a
fortitude worthy of Uncle Turkey.